Overcoming
Evil
in the Last Days
Expanded Edition with Study Guide

Overcoming
Evil
in the Last Days
Expanded Edition with Study Guide

RICK JOYNER

DESTINY IMAGE® PUBLISHERS, INC.

P.O. Box 310, Shippensburg, PA 17257-0310

"Speaking to the Purposes of God for This Generation and for the Generations to Come."

This book and all other Destiny Image, Revival Press, Mercy Place, Fresh Bread, Destiny Image Fiction, and Treasure House books are available at Christian bookstores and distributors worldwide.

For a U.S. bookstore nearest you, call 1-800-722-6774.

For more information on foreign distributors, call 717-532-3040.

Or reach us on the Internet: www.destinyimage.com.

ISBN 10: 0-7684-2833-5

ISBN 13: 978-0-7684-2833-9

Previously published as ISBN 0-7684-2178-0

For Worldwide Distribution, Printed in the U.S.A.

1 2 3 4 5 6 7 8 9 10 11 / 13 12 11 10 09

CONTENTS

Introduction

SATAN'S CORD OF THREE STRANDS

In this book, we will examine three of the most powerful evil strongholds that together bind and control fallen humankind—racism, witchcraft, and the religious spirit. As Ecclesiastes 4:12 states, **"And if one can overpower him who is alone, two can resist him. A cord of three strands is not quickly torn apart."** These three, working together in a deadly alliance, can be seen at the root of almost all the death and destruction that has been the bane of human history. This is satan's **"cord of three strands"** that is very difficult to break. It is crucial for us to understand these strongholds because, without this understanding, we cannot comprehend the world in which we live, particularly the ultimate conflict between good and evil that will mark the end of this age.

I have previously addressed these strongholds in articles and have also written a series of booklets on spiritual strongholds. However, this book is a more in-depth study. As we seek understanding of the ultimate evil forces, we must always keep in mind that it is the truth that sets us free (see John 8:32). Our goal is to understand not just the evil, but even more so, the counterforce of truth that alone can break the power of evil. Truth breaks the power of evil by displacing it. Our goal is not just to stop doing evil, but to do good and to thereby bear fruit for the Kingdom of God.

As the Lord taught in Luke 11:24-26, when an unclean spirit goes out of a person, it will try to return if the place that it left is not occupied. Not only will it return, but it will also bring seven other evil spirits more powerful than itself. Therefore, our goal must always be to not only cast out the evil, but to fill the place it occupied with the truth of the Holy Spirit. The best way to do this is to drive out the evil and deception with the truth—the counterpower to the deception. We therefore are not just trying to reveal what is wrong, but to reveal God's righteousness and truth that is the counter to it. We then want to sink our roots deeper and deeper into His truth so that it is not just a concept that we believe, but the nature of who we are.

It is for this reason that you will notice some redundancies in this study. Repetition is required for retention; thus the goal of this study is not just to illuminate the evil, but to drive the seed of truth deeper and deeper into our hearts so that it can never be lost or stolen. Just as a healthy tree has roots growing below the surface that are as extensive as the branches above it, we want to be on the inside all that our outward actions reveal. We want truth in our innermost being (see Ps. 51:6). Then the fruit that we produce will not only be abundant, but be of the highest quality and strength.

As the Lord teaches in the parable of the sower, every seed of truth will be tested before it can bear fruit (see Matt. 13). Our goal is to not only pass the tests, but to bear much fruit. We do this by first getting free ourselves, and then by also setting others free of these evil strongholds. Christians are called to be the ultimate freedom fighters.

As we begin to understand each of the ultimate strongholds addressed in this book, we must also understand how they tend to work together. For example, if we start to experience freedom from racism or a control spirit, which is a form of witchcraft, the devil will usually send a religious spirit to encourage us to unrighteously judge others who are still bound by racism or the control spirit. In this way, the religious spirit builds another stronghold, one of pride, that will make a way for the racism and control spirits to return. Then, when these strongholds are empowered by the religious spirit, they become much more powerful than before.

Because of these interrelationships and cross strategies of the enemy, it is important for us to study all of these together. We must always keep in mind that we are not warring against flesh and blood, but against the evil forces that are controlling people (see Eph. 6:12). God gives His grace to the humble (see James 4:6); so we must endeavor to always walk in the humility of knowing that, though we have been given grace, we are not any better than those who do not yet have it. In fact, we are the servants of those who are not yet free, servant warriors who have been sent to set them free.

It is entirely understandable that confronting such issues could be alarming to you. However, some foolishly think it is better to remain ignorant of such things and to let others do the spiritual warfare thing. But those who think this way are the ones who will inevitably fall into the worst snares of the devil. Truth is fundamental to Christianity, and if we are true followers of Christ, we will be in pursuit of truth, regardless of the responsibilities that it brings upon us. It is our calling to rule and reign with Him (see 2 Tim. 2:12), and our training for reigning is during this life. The true Christian life is precisely all about growing in truth and using the divinely powerful weapons that we have been given to destroy the works of the devil.

If the Lord had wanted things to be easy for us, He could have bound the devil immediately after His resurrection. We must understand that the battle that we are engaged in is a good fight. There can be no victories without a battle. We have been entrusted with divinely powerful weapons that no evil can stand against. The Bible is God's plan, and if you have not done so yet, read the end of the story—we win! You are on the side that cannot lose. The battle is for our sakes, so that we can grow in the character and faith that will decide the degree of authority that we are entrusted with in the age to come.

The purpose of this book is to shine light into the darkness, which is the root of satan's power over humankind. Because the devil dwells in darkness, truth or illumination will begin to break his power over our lives. One Christian who walks in truth can be the most powerful force on earth. One such Christian is the greatest terror in hell. That is what you are called to be. If you are walking in the light, you will fear no evil, but all evil will be in fear of you. As we are promised in James 4:7, if we resist the devil he will not only leave us alone, he will *flee* from us. Far too many Christians spend their lives desperately trying to ward off the attacks of the enemy. It is time that we arise in the authority that we have been given so that we can put him on the defensive. That is your calling.

You have a promise in First Peter 5:6-10:

> **Therefore humble yourselves under the mighty hand of God, that He may exalt you at the proper time, casting all your anxiety on Him, because He cares for you. Be of sober spirit, be on the alert. Your adversary, the devil, prowls around like a roaring lion, seeking someone to devour. But resist him, firm in your faith, knowing that the same experiences of suffering are being accomplished by your brethren who are in the world. After you have suffered for a little while, the God of all grace, who called you to His eternal glory in Christ, will Himself perfect, confirm, strengthen and establish you.**

Part I

RACISM

Chapter One

THE ULTIMATE POWERS OF EVIL

We first address the stronghold of racism because its power is rooted in two of the ultimate yokes that hold people in bondage and that, therefore, are the roots of the evil one's power. When they are broken, it is much easier to be set free from every other yoke of bondage.

Racism is one of the ultimate strongholds that binds humankind, and it is the primary stronghold that empowers the spirit of death. It is the linchpin yoke of bondage that empowers satan's "cord of three strands." For this reason, he seeks to impose it on every church and movement that is making a spiritual advance. It has been an effective strategy since most in history have fallen to this great evil in at least one of its forms. Because deception is deceptive, those who are bound by it often believe they are the most free from the prejudices of racism.

You may think I am carrying this problem a bit too far, but both the Scriptures and history confirm it. First, we must understand that racism is not just about race. We must also understand how racism is rooted in two of the most basic evil powers that have controlled humankind since The Fall—fear and pride. A person becomes a racist either because of pride in the flesh or because of fear of those who are different, both of which are a thick veil over the human soul. Racism is one of the most powerful of the evil world rulers.

The Sign

The harvest will come at the end of the age and will be the reaping of everything that has been sown in man, both the good and the evil. Fear and pride will come to full maturity in man at the end. When Jesus was asked about the signs that would accompany the end of the age He said, **"...nation will rise against nation, and kingdom against kingdom..."** (Matt. 24:7). The word that is translated "nation" in this text is the Greek word *ethnos*, from which we derive our English word "ethnic." This makes it clear that a prominent sign at the end of this age and His return will be ethnic conflict. In fulfillment of this Scripture, one of the greatest issues now facing the world and the Church is ethnic conflict.

The world is losing control of its racial problems. The cause is a spiritual power that no legislation or human agency can stop. Only that which is bound in Heaven can be bound upon the earth (see Matt. 16:19). If the Church does not face this problem—overcoming the racism within our own ranks so that we can take spiritual authority over it—the world will soon fall into an abyss of chaos, destruction, and suffering of unprecedented proportions—all because of racial conflict. As the Lord stated in His discourse about the end, as recorded in Luke 21:25-26:

> **There will be signs in sun and moon and stars, and on the earth dismay among nations [ethnos], in perplexity at the roaring of the sea and the waves, men fainting from fear and the expectation of the things which are coming upon the world; for the powers of the heavens will be shaken.**

We read in Revelation 17:15, **"The waters which you saw...are peoples and multitudes and nations and tongues."** In the text from Luke, we see that the **"roaring of the sea and the waves"** is the result of the turmoil among the *ethnos,* or ethnic conflicts. This will become so great that people will faint from the fear of it.

This problem will not go away with time, but it will increase. The longer we wait to confront this stronghold, the more powerful it will become. Pressure is now building in almost every world-class city, but when it erupts, it will not be confined to only the cities. It is rising up between cultures and nations, with pressure building to the boiling point. Ancient cultural wounds and offenses are motivating the politics of many nations. We can point to almost every war and conflict in the world today as being rooted in racism of some form.

Racism is like fuel that has been poured over the dry tinder of the world—the only thing it lacks in any place is the striking of a match to ignite it. The frenzy of the fire of racism can be unprecedented in releasing demented human passions. After the 1994 murders of nearly one million people in Rwanda over the period of a few months, some of those who were the most involved in the slaughter of thousands of people said that they did not even remember doing it. They were not denying their guilt, as they sat covered in blood, but they explained that it was like something had come over them and they were just carried along by it. They were right.

What happened in Rwanda was one of satan's dress rehearsals for what he wants to release on the earth. If we are arrogant enough to believe that we live in a country too civilized for such a thing to happen, that very pride could be the only door that the devil needs. Of all the nations in Africa, Rwanda was the one where such a thing was least expected. Ninety percent Christian, the Rwandans were considered the most peaceful, loving people in Africa. Nazi Germany was also considered a Christian nation. How did the devil take them over? This is a question we must answer.

The Higher Power

The Lord has demonstrated His power to calm the storm and the sea. King David declared of Him, **"By awesome deeds You answer us in righteousness, O God of our salvation...who stills the roaring of the seas, the roaring of their waves, and the tumult of the peoples"** (Ps. 65:5,7).

The Lord will again stand up and calm the roaring sea with His Word. The Lord came to destroy the works of the devil (see 1 John 3:8), and He has sent us with this same purpose. We are not here to watch as spectators, but we are to stand against the darkness and to push it back. We must, however, know our enemy—racism is one of the ultimate enemies of the truth, the Gospel, and humankind. It is an enemy that we must face in the Church. It is an enemy that we will conquer.

Racism is not just a demon, or even a principality—it is a "world ruler." It is one of the most powerful strongholds on the earth, and it has sown more death and destruction than any other. The most deadly wars in history, including World War II, were ignited by racism. This powerful spirit prepares the way for and empowers the spirit of death. The apostle Paul understood that, when the ultimate racial barrier, the division between Jew and Gentile, is overcome and they are grafted together in Christ, it will mean nothing less than **"life from the dead"** (Rom. 11:15), or the overcoming of death.

The Roots of Racism

As stated, there are two foundations of racism. The first is pride. One of its most base forms is pride in the flesh, or judging others based on the externals, which is the ultimate form of pride. In its basic form, pride is simply the statement that we feel sufficient within ourselves and that we do not really need God or others. This creates an obvious barrier between ourselves and others.

The second foundation of racism is fear. Insecurity is a result of The Fall and the separation between God and man. The insecure are afraid of those who are different and those whom they cannot control. Racism is a powerful and deeply interwoven combination of both pride and fear.

Fear breaks relationships (trust is the bridge that establishes relationships). You can have love and even genuine forgiveness, but if you do not have trust, a relationship is not possible. Fear and pride tear down the trust that makes a relationship possible, therefore creating division.

Breaking the Power of Evil

The cross of Christ confronts and overcomes both pride and insecurity. The Holy Spirit was sent to convict the world of sin because it is the revelation of our sin that drives us to the cross to find grace and forgiveness. This destroys our pride and establishes our dependency on the Savior, which also restores our trust in Him. The deeper the cross works in us, the more humble and secure we will become in His love. When we, who are so foreign to God's nature, are accepted back into Him by His grace, we receive a tolerance for those who are different from us. Those who become spiritual begin to judge from a spiritual perspective, not from a fleshly perspective.

> **Therefore from now on we recognize no one according to the flesh; even though we have known Christ according to the flesh, yet now we know Him in this way no longer. Therefore if anyone is in Christ, he is a new creature; the old things passed away; behold, new things have come** (2 Corinthians 5:16-17).

The Church should not judge others according to the color of their skin or their cultural background. We must learn to see by the Spirit and to judge only by the Spirit, just as it was said of Jesus:

> **The Spirit of the Lord will rest on Him, the spirit of wisdom and understanding, the spirit of counsel and strength, the spirit of knowledge and the fear of the Lord. And He will delight in the fear of the Lord, and He will not judge by what His eyes see, nor make a decision by what His ears hear** (Isaiah 11:2-3).

If we are going to walk as He walked, we too must learn to see and hear as He did. This is the great lesson of the two men on the road to Emmaus. The resurrected Christ appeared to these disciples and preached to them about Himself for quite awhile. This was Christ preaching Christ—it will never be more anointed than that! Yet they still could not recognize Him. Why? Because **"He appeared in a different form"** (Mark 16:12).

One of the primary reasons why we miss the Lord when He tries to draw near to us is because we tend to know even the Lord according to a form rather than by the Spirit. If we are Charismatics, we tend to only recognize Him when He comes to us through a Charismatic. If we are a Baptist, we tend to only know Him when He comes to us through a Baptist. However, He will usually approach us in a form that is different from what we are used to. He did so with His own disciples after His resurrection. This is because He is always seeking for us to know Him through the Spirit, not through externals.

The Lord declared: **"For I say to you, from now on you will not see Me until you say, 'Blessed is He who comes in the name of the Lord'"** (Matt. 23:39). We will not see Him until we learn to bless those whom He sends to us, regardless of the form in which they come. Even Israel did not recognize the Lord when He came to them in a form that they were not expecting. This is not a new problem with God's people, but it remains a serious one.

The Glory of Diversity

The Church is called to have, and to be a reflection of, the answers to the most fundamental human problems. Racism is one of the most basic and deadly problems in human history, and its power is increasing greatly at this time. However, the Lord declared: **"My house shall be called a house of prayer for all the nations [ethnos]..."** (Mark 11:17). The Church has not fulfilled her destiny until she truly becomes a house of prayer for all ethnic peoples. This makes the Church the ultimate antithesis to the evil of racism.

Paul said that **"tongues are for a sign" (1 Cor. 14:22).** What sign? The sign that the Church is to be the antithesis to the tower of Babel—where humankind's languages were scattered and where people were separated into different races and cultures. We see the first great demonstration of this on the Day of Pentecost, at the very birth of the Church.

> **Now there were Jews living in Jerusalem, devout men from every nation [ethnos] under heaven. And when this sound occurred, the crowd came together, and were bewildered because each one of them was hearing them speak in his own language** (Acts 2:5-6).

The Church is the place where people will be unified again, regardless of race, culture, language, and so forth. Is it not interesting that Jews from every *ethnos* heard and understood in one language? Jesus is the Word of God, or God's communication to us. When people see His glory, when He is lifted up, all people will be drawn to Him and will understand with one heart again (see John 12:32). The Church that truly worships Him will be a demonstration of that. Paul told the Galatians that, in the Church, every convert, from any cultural background or gender, has an equal standing before God.

> **For all of you who were baptized into Christ have clothed yourselves with Christ. There is neither Jew nor Greek, there is neither slave nor free man, there is neither male nor female; for you are all one in Christ Jesus** (Galatians 3:27-28).

There may be differences in our standing before God in such things as governmental authority or within a specific ministry, but that has nothing to do with race, gender, or cultural background. Even the newest born-again Christian can go as boldly before the throne of God as the greatest preacher in the world. God does not show partiality, and if we are walking by His Spirit, neither will we.

This is just the beginning of our study of this ultimate enemy of the Church and humankind. Before we proceed, stop and ask the Lord if there are any roots of this evil in your own heart. If there are, ask Him to help you to see them and to repent of them.

The gates of hell are the enemy's access points into our lives. Racism is one of the biggest doors that the evil one now has into the world and into our individual lives. Therefore, those who escape the shackles of racism possess the power to shut the gates of hell and to become some of the greatest threats to the power of the evil one in this world. To be free of racism is to replace fear and pride with humility and faith, two of the greatest powers on earth. That is our goal in this study. In the next chapter, we will examine the major tentacles of racism's power and control.

Chapter Two

THE TYRANNY OF THE FAMILIAR

The psychological problem called "the tyranny of the familiar" is considered by many to be one of the most difficult to understand. It is a powerful yoke that can crush the potential and personality of human beings. It is one of the strongest spiritual yokes that binds fallen human beings and the Church. This yoke has baffled psychologists, but it has baffled Christian leaders for even longer, sometimes turning new Christians into "old wineskins" in a matter of weeks, making them too rigid and inflexible to receive new truth.

Likewise, psychologists cannot understand why a high percentage of girls who grow up in the home of an alcoholic father, regardless of the pain and torment that this caused, will marry a heavy drinker. Why do abused women risk their lives to protect their abusers? Great cultures, such as Germany was before World War II, will expend themselves and even perish while following demented leaders. As incomprehensible as it seems, the familiar, although painful and dangerous, is still more desirable to them than the unfamiliar, even though it offers much more hope.

This is the same yoke that keeps many ethnic groups from breaking out of their sociological and economic barriers. In spite of all of the talk and genuine frustrations, most people are afraid of change. Why is it that we so easily come under bondage to the familiar? Basically it is because we tend to put our security in our environment instead of in the Lord.

To institute true change, we must build a strong trust as a bridge out of our situation, which usually takes more time and effort than most people are willing to sacrifice. This is not a new problem. We even see this bondage in the children of Israel when they preferred the flesh pots of Egypt over the supernatural provision of God. Jeremiah 48:11-12 also addresses this issue in relation to the nation of Moab.

> **"Moab has been at ease since his youth; he has also been undisturbed, like wine on its dregs, and he has not been emptied from vessel to vessel, nor has he gone into exile. Therefore he retains his flavor, and his aroma has not changed. Therefore behold, the days are coming," declares the Lord, "when I will send to him those who tip vessels, and they will tip him over, and they will empty his vessels and shatter his jars."**

The Lord was talking about change when describing being emptied from vessel to vessel. This was how wine was purified in those times. It was poured into a vessel and allowed to sit for a time. As it sat, the impurities would settle to the bottom. Then it was poured into another vessel and allowed to sit so that the remaining impurities could again settle. Consequently, the more the wine had been emptied from vessel to vessel, the more pure it became. Because Moab had not been subjected to the purifying changes, the "wine" of that nation was impure; therefore, the Lord vowed to pour it out.

Every time the wine was poured into a new vessel, it was unsettled—there was commotion and stirring, which would bring the impurities to the surface. Whenever we are thrust into change, many things will begin to surface in our lives. This is a reason why the Lord often allows radical changes, which are almost always disconcerting, to impact our lives. Usually we will see very quickly just how much we have trusted in the "vessel" we occupy instead of in the Lord. But we will settle down again, and we will be more pure. Change is cleansing. That is one reason why the Lord kept Israel moving most of the time in the wilderness.

The Wine of America

Now let us look at how this applies in a national situation. A good example is found as we look at the problems of African Americans. African American crime and violence in the inner cities can usually be traced to family problems. Unfortunately, a low percentage of African American families have a father at home. Of course, some of the great fathers in America are also African American, but in general, there is a serious problem in many of these families that can be traced to the lack of a strong father. What is the root of this problem? In one word—slavery.

Think about what the fathers in slave families had to endure. It is difficult to comprehend what it was like for a father to go to sleep each night knowing that he could be sold the next day and never see his family again. His wife, children, or both, could be sold, and he would never even know where they went. What would that do to the family? Fathers, mothers, and children alike could not truly give their hearts to each other because of the terrible pain that they would inevitably suffer. The tearing apart of these families became the root of some of the great social problems in America today. It is a social wound that must be addressed and healed, or we will pay an increasingly high price until it is much more than we can afford.

The Diabolical Root

In 1712, a slave owner in the West Indies named Wilson Lynch wrote a letter to the British colonies in Virginia devising a strategy to break up slave families and loyalties, thus keeping them from rising in rebellion. He projected that, when their family loyalties were destroyed, the only loyalty that the slaves would have would be to their owners. Lynch also declared that, when this strategy was implemented, it would destroy the fabric of those families for several hundred years. Of course, this was a letter from hell, and the diabolical prophecy came true. African American women have had to be both father and mother to their families for centuries, and they are having a difficult time accepting fathers in their rightful place. Fathers are having just as difficult of a time taking their place.

Those who face this problem and overcome it are able to become some of the greatest fathers of all; and African American families who are united are rising to become some of the great and noble families. This is why the television series *Roots* had such a powerful impact on America. It addressed the core problem like few movies, books, or pieces of art ever have, and it called a great and noble people to find their roots in their families again.

If any other people had suffered the same historic problems as the African American race, they too would be having the same problems that African Americans are having now, and maybe worse. However, I have heard many white leaders (unbelievably) say that we would have no inner city problems if African Americans just had some ambition. What impact do they think the drudgery, toil, and oppression of slavery had on their work ethic? Such deep cultural wounds cannot be healed without the intervention of the cross.

African Americans were subjected to slavery for the same reason that the Lord allowed Israel to become slaves in Egypt—they have a destiny with God. When they come into this destiny, the rest of America is going to be very thankful for this great, noble, and free people in our midst. It is the destiny of African Americans to carry freedom to a new level. This will be true freedom with the dignity and honor that God created people to have.

The Power for Healing

We know that it is by the Lord's stripes that we are healed (see 1 Pet. 2:24), and we receive the authority for healing in the very place where we are wounded. African Americans are going to embrace the cross, receive healing for their wounds, and start loving white people with such a power that we will all be set free by that love.

The Uncle Tom of *Uncle Tom's Cabin* truly was a prophetic figure. Uncle Tom is understandably offensive to African Americans who have not yet been to the cross, but he is a type of Christ to those who have. In spite of all the abuse that he suffered at the hands of his owners, he was freer than they were, and he was willing to use his great freedom to lay down his own life to bring about his owners' salvation. When African Americans have been fully healed, they will bring revival and true spiritual liberty to the whole nation—even and especially to their oppressors.

The inner cities of America will ultimately become the inner sanctuary of God's tabernacle—the place where His glory and presence dwells. The greatest move of God that America has yet to experience will come out of the inner cities. The suburban churches may have the gold, but the inner-city churches will make them jealous with the glory. Those who are wise will take the gold that they have and use it to build a tabernacle for the Lord that is not made with hands, but with people.

The National Call

America is made up of people from every other nation, which is the foundation of our greatness, but it is also the foundation of our greatest problems. Even so, we have the potential to touch something of the glory of God that few other nations have. Our nation has the setting of another great Pentecost, which was a place where people came to dwell **"from every nation under heaven"** (Acts 2:5). We actually have the greatest opportunity to overcome and demonstrate the solution to one of the world's most deadly problems. When our great day comes, we must also be as those of the first Pentecost, in which the Church was **"all with one accord"** (Acts 2:1 KJV), or in unity.

America is at the threshold of either her greatest victory or greatest failure. This powerful last-day stronghold will either be defeated on our shores, or it will defeat us. America will rise to even greater heights as a nation and world leader, or she will fall like every previous great world power. If we do not embrace this glorious potential, we will be destroyed by the problems.

When the Lord described the judgment, He said that He was going to separate the nations into "sheep" and "goats" (see Matt. 25:31-46). The sheep will inherit His Kingdom, and the goats will inherit eternal punishment. He said that they would be distinguished by these characteristics: the sheep were those who, when He was thirsty, gave Him water; when He was hungry, gave Him food; and when He was a stranger, took Him in. When the sheep inquired about when they did this, He answered: **"Truly I say to you, to the extent that you did it to one of these brothers of Mine, even the least of them, you did it to Me"** (Matt. 25:40).

One of the primary issues on which we will be judged will be our oneness with those who are different from us. Even the nations will be separated in this way. We know that at the end many nations will go to a terrible destruction, but we also know that some of the kingdoms of this world will become the kingdoms of our Lord (see Rev. 11:15). The nations that will be judged as "sheep," so as to enter His Kingdom, will be those who are open to foreigners and strangers.

This is a fundamental issue on which we will all be judged, and it is a reason why the Lord has bestowed His blessings upon America, and a number of other nations, to the degree that He has. Because racism deals with two of the most basic issues of the human heart—fear and pride—confronting these issues is one of the greatest opportunities that we have for entering His Kingdom.

Humility is a basic characteristic that enables us to be open to those who are different from us. It also helps others to lower their defenses against us. Because God **"gives grace to the humble"** (James 4:6), overcoming this problem opens us up like nothing else to the grace of God. When we add Christian love to this and become devoted to building up one another rather than tearing each other down, we are building upon the foundation of the Kingdom.

Chapter Three

HEALING CULTURAL WOUNDS

Cultural sins are passed down from generation to generation until people recognize them, humble themselves, and repent for the sins of their fathers. This prayer of repentance, so often seen in the Old Testament, was usually prayed by the most righteous men, like Daniel, who had nothing to do with the sin. They simply understood this principle and were willing to stand in the gap for their people. This was the foundation of the cross and is the true nature of Christ and those who would be Christlike.

Biblical repentance is more than just saying we are sorry or even feeling sorry—it is turning from our evil ways. The white church in the South was one of the bastions that gave birth to demented theologies and philosophies that justified and perpetuated slavery. The Southern Baptist Convention was actually born in an attempt to justify and perpetuate the institution of slavery. Even though the Southern Baptist Convention of today is quite different from the original convention—and it is important to note that there have been many Southern Baptists on the very forefront of the war against racism—there is a reason why 11 o'clock on Sunday morning is still the most segregated hour of the week. There are still bastions of racism in the Southern Baptist Convention and most other denominations and movements within the Church.

This is not meant to point the finger at any single group. The whole Church is one of the bastions of this most powerful stronghold of the enemy—racism. That is one main reason why we have so many denominations. However, the Church will someday be free, and Southern Baptists will help to lead us out of this terrible darkness that is now sweeping the earth. The Southern Baptists are on the verge of a great revival, and it will be ignited by their unyielding assault on this terrible, evil power of racism.

The white Southern Baptist Church should have had the honor of doing what Martin Luther King, Jr. did—taking the leadership in this great battle against the world ruler of racism. Even so, the Southern Baptist Church will take up the fight and will ultimately lead it. The Lord delights in redemption—it is His primary business. He will delight in taking what was meant for evil in the Southern Baptist Convention and using it for good, destroying the very evil that tried to use His Church this way.

The Light of the Church

Racism is one of the world's most serious problems, and the Church must show the world the answer to this problem. However, we will not have spiritual authority over the world's problems if we have the same strongholds within ourselves. We must recognize that the Church today is still one of the most powerful bastions of racism, and it is still one of the most segregated institutions in the world. There are some notable exceptions to this, but generally the presence of racism in the Church is very real.

Spiritual bigotry is just as prevalent as the natural form. Spiritual racism is at work when we judge other churches, movements, or people as inferior or frightening because they are not a part of our group. This spiritual form of racism is a root cause of many of the present divisions and denominations in the Body of Christ.

When Paul listed the qualifications for elders in the Church, he specified that they must be "hospitable" (see Titus 1:8). In the original Greek, this Scripture actually states, "one who shows hospitality to aliens or foreigners." Basically he was saying that to be a leader of the Church, a believer had to be open to those who were different. This is fundamental to true spiritual leadership. One who cannot value those who are different is either too proud or too insecure to be in Church leadership.

The Nature of Our Unity

While the whole world is degenerating into increasing chaos from its ethnic conflicts, the Church will become increasingly unified. However, we must understand our unity. This does not mean that we all become the same or submit to the same organizational structure, just as a husband can never become one with his wife by trying to make her a man. Our unity is based on the *recognition* and *appreciation* of our differences.

The whole creation reflects the Lord's love for diversity. He makes every snowflake, every tree, and every person *different*. He also desires to make every church different. These differences, however, are not designed to create conflict but to complement one another. It is only because of our continued distance from the Lord and our resulting insecurity that we view these differences as threats.

I am not implying that there will be no doctrinal and procedural differences in conflict between churches and movements. We must also understand that the true unity of the Church will not come by compromising our convictions. Even so, most of the differences that have brought conflict and division in the Church are not serious enough for us to divide over. In many cases, those whom we resist the most are the very ones we need the most to give *proper* balance and perspective to our vision of the truth.

During my 30 plus years in the Church, I have never witnessed a single division that was really based on a genuine commitment to truth. Men may have used doctrine or procedure as an excuse to divide from each other, but the real reason behind every split that I have witnessed was territorial preservation. This is a most deadly and selfish evil in the Church and a major foundation of our spiritual racism.

As stated, racism empowers the spirit of death, and this spirit has probably killed more churches and movements than any other enemy.

Until we are free of this enemy, we will not have spiritual authority over it in human affairs. The only answer for us and the world is the cross. At the cross, the dividing walls are taken down and we are free to come into true unity.

Another of the most significant barriers in the world today is the one between men and women. This is also related to racism. One of the enemy's primary strategies against humanity is to blur the distinctions between men and women. Why would he do this if he is trying to divide us? The reason is because a husband cannot become one with his wife by making her into a man. Neither can a man become the true man that he was created to be until he learns to properly relate to women, recognizing and appreciating their differences.

Men will be unable to have a true perception of the world or anything else, including the Lord, until they are open to the woman's perspective about these things. The same is true for women. We must take our different perspectives and put them together if we are to see and understand clearly. Therefore, to walk in truth, we need each other. A woman will never be the lady that she has been created to be without learning to relate to men properly. Deep wounds remain within each, but there is healing for all at the cross. There is no true healing anywhere else.

Likewise, Charismatic, Pentecostal, Baptist, Methodist (or any other denomination) believers will never fulfill their destinies without a proper relationship to the rest of the Body of Christ. Even though the high priest of Israel was from the tribe of Levi, he carried the stones that represented all the different tribes on his chest. This was to symbolize that those who walked in the high calling must carry all of God's people on their hearts.

Only when we have been delivered from our own spiritual and ethnic conflicts will we be called **"a house of prayer for all nations"** (Isaiah 56:7 NKJV), which is our fundamental calling. The times are about to press us into the desperation that is obviously required for us to do this. Let us not waste a day, for those who do not overcome the world will be overcome by it. When we begin to carry the cross, there is no spirit in this world that will not be subject to us. The cross has overcome the world, and when we embrace it, we too will overcome the world.

There will never be true unity until we can see each other with the Lord's eyes, hear each other with His ears, and love each other with His heart. Every human problem in the world is impossible to overcome until we embrace the cross. But how can we expect people to do this until the Church does? We can only bear true spiritual fruit to the degree that we are abiding in the Vine. The stronger our union is with Him, the more fruit we will bear.

The Lord Jesus did not judge by what He saw with His natural eyes or heard with His natural ears. His judgment was determined by what the Father revealed to Him. We cannot expect to walk in truth if we continue to receive our discernment from the secular press, the evening news, or even what we see with our own eyes at times. There is always a story behind the story that only God knows, and He will reveal it to us if we turn to Him for our understanding.

We know that the Lord resists the proud but gives His grace to the humble. One of the surest signs of true humility is being teachable, and a sign of ultimate humility is our willingness to be taught by someone who is different from us. This is why racial differences present one of the most potent opportunities for both the Lord and the devil. The devil uses it to create further division by releasing pride and fear. The Lord's purpose is always for us to grow in humility, faith, and love. Which will it be for us?

Chapter Four

A PRACTICAL STRATEGY

In Deuteronomy 10:18-19, the Israelites were commanded to love the alien who was in their midst. In Deuteronomy 31:12, they were commanded to teach the alien. There is an important revelation in the sequence of these Scriptures—*we must love someone before we can teach them*. Again, true spiritual authority is founded upon love.

America is the most powerful nation on earth at this time. An unbiased student of history would almost certainly consider it also the greatest and most benevolent power in history. What other nation would rebuild and restore its enemies the way that America did after World War II? What nation is ever on the scene of a crisis or natural disaster anywhere in the world before Americans? America is the most respected and emulated nation on earth. At the same time, it is also probably the most despised nation on earth. Why?

This hatred of America is not simply out of jealousy; there is another basis to this hatred. Although it may be almost entirely unintentional, we continually offend and insult other cultures, sometimes even with our benevolence. Because we are a nation that is truly made up of those from every other nation, we should most certainly be the last to do this.

At last count, almost 60 prime ministers and leaders of other nations have been educated in the United States, and yet a high percentage of these were anti-American in their policy. The Japanese military leader who planned the attack on Pearl Harbor and the admiral who commanded the attack force were both educated at Harvard University! When they came to America, one of their goals was to make American friends, but they were shunned by the American students. How could history have been changed if we had treated these men differently?

Between 200,000 and 300,000 foreigners are presently being educated in the United States. These students are usually the "cream of the crop" of their nations. Many are from nations where it is against the law to preach the Gospel. We can reach the world without ever leaving home just by showing hospitality to the foreigners who are presently on our college campuses. They are usually isolated and lonely, and many of them have nowhere to go during holidays. Because of these circumstances, their time in the United States is a negative experience. Many of them will one day be the leaders of their nations—some even prime ministers or foreign ministers. If churches that are located near campuses would reach out to these foreigners, the world could be greatly impacted.

The Ultimate Racist Barrier

The ultimate racist barrier, with regard to spiritual power, is the barrier between Jew and Gentile. This separation is by God's design. The Jew is the natural seed of Abraham, and the Church is the spiritual seed. Together they are meant to represent the heavens and the earth, which is why the promise to Abraham was that his seed would be **"as the stars of the heavens and as the sand which is on the seashore"** (Gen. 22:17). When the barrier between Jew and Gentile is overcome, it will signal the overcoming of the gulf between the spiritual and earthly realm, so that God, who is Spirit, may establish His eternal habitation with humankind.

The Jew is the embodiment of the humanistic spirit. They are a barometer of humanity—embattled within and without. As Paul said, **"From the standpoint of the gospel they are enemies for your sake"** (Rom. 11:28). They were hardened, or made hard to reach, *for the sake of the Gospel*. That is, the Jew represents the "acid test" of our message. Until we have a Gospel that will make the Jews jealous, we do not really have it right. This means not only having it right doctrinally, but also practically in the way that it changes us, which is reflected in our preaching of the Gospel. Perhaps this is why we are exhorted to preach the Gospel to the Jews first, because when we preach to the Jews, we will quickly find out the quality of our message.

The wounds that have been afflicted upon Jews by the Church are some of the deepest and most tragic in history, which makes our job to reach them much more difficult. It will take an unprecedented humility on the part of the Church, which will enable the Lord to extend His unprecedented grace to trust us with an unprecedented anointing to reach the Jews. This is precisely God's plan. We cannot fulfill our commission as the Church without the Jews. They must be grafted back into God's Kingdom, which will require an unprecedented anointing. But first the Church has to be in a place of such humility and grace that every racist barrier in us is overcome. That is why Paul confidently affirmed that, when this happened, it would release the ultimate grace on humankind: **"For if their rejection is the reconciliation of the world, what will their acceptance be but life from the dead"** (Rom. 11:15). The spirit of death and the racism that empowers it will be overcome when the Jew and Gentile have been grafted into the Vine together. Therefore, the Church must place the overcoming of racist barriers as a top priority. What can we do to build the bridges of trust between us?

The New Creation

The time period in which the Lord dealt almost exclusively with the Jews was about 2,000 years. The time of the Gentiles has now been about 2,000 years. We are coming to the time when the Jew and the Gentile are being grafted into one new creation through Christ.

True unity is found in diversity, not in conformity. Converted Israel will not be like the Church. The Church is very far from being what God created her to be, and so is Israel. When they are truly joined together, neither will be as they are now. We desperately need what the born-again Jew will bring into the Church. This does not imply a returning to the Law; rather, the Church has not yet demonstrated on earth what the true new creation is. This union of the natural and spiritual seed of Abraham is required before it can be seen. This is the best wine, which the Lord has saved for last.

Many in the Church have embraced a "replacement theology," which replaces all of the present purposes of God for Israel with the Church. Others have embraced a "replacement, replacement theology" which replaces the Church with Israel. Both cloud the ultimate purpose for Israel and the Church. In the Book of Romans, which is the most explicit book of New Covenant theology in the Scriptures, Paul clearly established God's purpose for each. He also warned against becoming **"...arrogant toward the [natural] branches..."** (Rom. 11:18). He added, **"...Do not be conceited, but fear; for if God did not spare the natural branches, He will not spare you, either"** (Rom. 11:20-21). This is an issue of such importance that it can cut us off from God's purpose.

This does not imply that we must accept everything that Israel does. It is also clearly unbiblical that the Jews can be grafted into the purpose of God in any way except through Christ. But speaking of the natural branches, Paul declared: **"I say then, God has not rejected His people, has He? May it never be..."** (Rom. 11:1). For God to reject natural Israel would be to impugn the very integrity of His promises to Abraham and throughout the entire Old Testament. Most of them cannot be attributed to anyone but the natural Jew. Paul asserted:

> **Then what advantage has the Jew? Or what is the benefit of circumcision? Great in every respect. First of all, that they were entrusted with the oracles of God. What then? If some did not believe, their unbelief will not nullify the faithfulness of God, will it? May it never be! Rather, let God be found true, though every man be found a liar, as it is written, "that you may be justified in**

your words, and prevail when you are judged" (Romans 3:1-4).

...From the standpoint of God's choice they are beloved for the sake of the fathers; for the gifts and the calling of God are irrevocable. For just as you once were disobedient to God, but now have been shown mercy because of their disobedience, so these also now have been disobedient, that because of the mercy shown to you they also may now be shown mercy. For God has shut up all in disobedience so that He may show mercy to all (Romans 11:28-32).

It will take extraordinary humility for the Church to fully see God's purpose in natural Israel, and it will take the same degree of humility for natural Israel to see God's purpose in the Church. It will happen; and when it does, it will release an unprecedented measure of God's grace to both.

Paul to the Gentiles and Peter to the Jews

Many believe that only converted Jews will be able to reach the Jews. This is contrary to God's purpose, as well as to the biblical testimony of how God reaches people. This was the reason why the Lord sent Peter to the Jews and Paul to the Gentiles. According to our modern mentality, the Lord made a mistake. Certainly in our minds, Paul, the Pharisee of Pharisees, would have been better able to relate to the Jews; and Peter, the simple fisherman, would obviously have been better able to reach the Gentiles. In the natural this is true, but our Gospel is not natural; it is spiritual, and the natural mind still cannot comprehend it.

The Lord sent Paul to the Gentiles because he was an offense to them. Therefore, the only way that Paul could fulfill his commission was to be utterly dependent on the Holy Spirit—which is the only way that the Gospel is truly empowered. Likewise, the only way that Peter could reach the Jews was to be utterly dependent on the Holy Spirit. This is true of us all! Natural affinities do not help the Gospel; they usually get in the way. **"That which is born of the flesh is flesh, and that which is born of the Spirit is spirit"** (John 3:6).

Just as the Lord humbled the Gentiles by sending them to Jews, He will humble the Jews by sending them to Gentiles. Of course, a few Jews will have some success in reaching their own people, but generally this will not be the way that they are reached. It is understandable that the heart of the Jewish convert longs to reach his own people, just as Paul's did. He was even willing to give up his own salvation (see Rom. 9:3-5). Even so, Paul could not reach the Jews because that was not his commission. The Gentile Church needs to take up the burden of reaching the Jews, and the Church desperately needs the converted Jews to help us reach them.

The Distortion of Reality

The news media is one of the primary tools being used by the enemy to sow deception and division between peoples. Although this may not be their intent, it is the end result. The news itself is a gross distortion of reality. Only the most extreme events make the news, and most of them are acts of violence. Good news does not sell, and even the good that makes the news is not a true perception of reality.

News of domestic violence is never balanced by news of the many happy families. The overwhelming majority of Americans today will do their jobs and go about their business in a normal manner, but none of that which is "normal" America will make the evening news. The news itself presents a distorted caricature of life in America or anywhere else.

Even the Christian media, trying to do an honest job of reporting the interesting events in the Church, often creates an unreal perception of Christianity for their own Christian readers or viewers. The average church in America is not like the churches that are newsworthy. The day-to-day ministries of the average church in a community are probably doing far more to accomplish a true advance for the Gospel, but it is rarely spectacular enough to make the news. Even so, these average churches are also a much more accurate reflection of the true state of Christianity today, for good or for bad.

Unfortunately, even when there is no intention to distort the facts, the very nature of the modern media distorts reality. Even family-oriented sitcoms project families where almost every action or statement is cute, funny, or dramatic. A normal family would make a very boring sitcom. When the average family compares their lives to those of the television family, they often become disappointed with what they have and who they are. The overall effect of this blurs reality and reduces our perceptions to "sound bites" in which we are being subtly trained only to respond to extremes.

Strongholds are basically lies that people believe. The more people who believe a falsehood, the more powerful that stronghold becomes. The enemy is using the media to sow a demented perception of almost everything. The result will be that more and more of the extremes projected by the media will become normal behavior. Only the Church, which has been given the Spirit of Truth, has the grace and power required to tear down these strongholds of misconception and false judgments. The divinely powerful weapons that we have been trusted with were given to us for the purpose of tearing down strongholds—and we must use them.

The Deception of Extremes

Satan has been very successful in causing and maintaining division between people by encouraging us to judge other people groups by their most extreme elements. Examples could include the way that some liberals look at conservatives and see the KKK or the way conservatives look at liberals and see communists. It is a primary strategy of the enemy to have us perceive one another through caricatures that the enemy has sown in our minds. This drives us further apart and decreases the possibility of unity, which the enemy fears so much.

Few Christians today are of the nature that was demonstrated by the crusaders, and the world tends to view us all according to the most extreme elements of the faith. We must also recognize that very few members of other religions or ethnic groups can be likened to the most extreme elements that we probably have viewed in the media.

Because the enemy's basic strategy is to sow division and misunderstanding by having us judge each other after projected images and caricatures, we must overcome this thought process by learning to judge other people after the Spirit and not after the flesh. We must not continue to receive our discernment, and in many cases, even our information, from the media, but from the Holy Spirit.

We Know in Part

Men need women, and women need men. Blacks need whites, and whites need blacks. Denominations need each other. We all need each other. It was for this purpose that First Corinthians 13:9 states, **"For we know in part and we prophesy in part."** Therefore, to have the complete picture, we must learn to put our little part together with the parts of others. We simply cannot make it through what is coming without unity, so we must learn what the rest of that chapter is about—love.

Love opens us up to seeing much more than we could otherwise see. Love is the foundation of all true vision and true prophecy. Anything but love will distort our vision. One of the tragic mistakes genuine prophetic people make is thinking that their little part is the whole vision. Thankfully, love opens our hearts to understand others and, therefore, receive from their perspective.

Chapter Five

THE TWO MINISTRIES

The Scriptures reveal that two acts occur continually before the throne of God—*intercession* and *accusation*. The conflict between these two is a focal point of the battle between the Kingdom of God and the kingdom of darkness. Because God has chosen to make the Church His dwelling place, and therefore the place of His throne, it is in the heart of the Church that this battle now rages.

Jesus **"always lives to make intercession"** (Heb. 7:25). The fundamental nature of Jesus is to be an intercessor, a priest. To the degree that we abide in Him, Jesus will use us to intercede. For this reason, His Church is called to be a **"house of prayer for all the nations"** (Mark 11:17).

Satan is called **"the accuser of our brethren...who accuses them before our God day and night"** (Rev. 12:10). To the degree that the enemy has access to our lives, he will use us to accuse and criticize the brethren. Like Adam and Eve, facing the two trees in the Garden, we must choose which of these we are going to partake of—intercession or accusation.

We may ask how satan could continue to accuse the saints before God if he has been thrown out of Heaven and no longer has access to the throne. The answer is that satan uses the saints, who do have access to the throne, to accomplish this diabolical work for him.

Satan's Greatest Victory

Satan is called by many titles, but certainly his most effective guise has been "accuser of the brethren." This title was given to him because of his effectiveness at getting brother to turn against brother. From the time that he entered the Garden to thwart the purpose of man (see Gen. 3:1), accusation has been his specialty. Even when there were just two brothers on earth, they could not get along. The presence of satan will always promote discord and division.

Satan's greatest victory over the Church is in turning the brethren against each other. *Accusation* has been his most effective and deadly tool in destroying the light, the power, and the witness of the Body of Christ. Our ability to accomplish our purpose in this world will be determined by the degree to which we can dispel our deadly enemy and learn to live for one another.

The greatest threat to satan's domain is the unity of the Church. The devil knows very well the awesome authority that Jesus has given to any two who will agree (see Matt. 18:19). He knows that, with agreement between just two saints, the Father will give them what they ask. He understands that one saint can put a thousand to flight but two of them together can put ten thousand to flight (see Deut. 32:30). Unity does not just increase our spiritual authority, it exponentially multiplies it. Unfortunately, the enemy understands all of this much better than the Church does.

The access the accuser has to most believers is through their insecurity. This drives them to become territorial or possessive. The insecure are threatened by anything that they cannot control. The accuser may use many seemingly noble justifications for his attacks on others, such as to protect the truth or the sheep, but rarely has there been a division in the Church that was not rooted in territorial- or self-preservation.

The greater the authority or influence that one has in the Church, the bigger the target he or she makes. Satan knows well that, if he can sow territorial or self-preservation in the heart of a spiritual leader, the leader will sow it in all of those under him and the division or sectarian spirit will become more destructive.

Ironically, the division that is caused by trying to protect our domains is the very thing that cuts us off from true spiritual authority and anointing. This ultimately results in us losing the very thing we are so desperately trying to preserve, which is an incontrovertible law of the spirit: **"For whoever wishes to save his life shall lose it; but whoever loses his life for My sake shall find it"** (Matt. 16:25). Isaiah addressed this issue in Isaiah 58:8-9:

> **Then your light will break out like the dawn, and your recovery will speedily spring forth; and your righteousness will go before you; the glory of the Lord will be your rear guard. Then you will call, and the Lord will answer; you will cry, and He will say, "Here I am." If you remove the yoke from your midst, the pointing of the finger and speaking wickedness.**

We are promised that, if we remove the yoke of criticism from our midst (portrayed as **"the pointing of the finger and speaking wickedness"**), our light will break out, our healing will come speedily, the glory of the Lord will follow us, and He will answer our prayers. There is possibly nothing that can so radically change the Church and the lives of individual believers as having our criticisms changed into intercession. Likewise, it is probable that the addiction to criticism is the main reason why there is so little light, so little healing, so little of the glory of the Lord, and so little answered prayer in the Church today.

Criticism Is Pride

Criticism is one of the ultimate manifestations of pride because when we criticize someone else, we assume we are superior to them. Pride brings that which any rational human being should fear the most—*God's resistance*. **"God resists the proud, but gives grace to the humble"** (James 4:6 NKJV). We would be better off having all of the demons in hell resisting us than God!

Pride caused the first Fall, and it has been a root in probably every fall from grace since. Peter's betrayal of the Lord is one of the great examples of how pride causes us to fall from grace. On the same night that Peter betrayed the Lord, he earlier charged a Roman cohort to defend his Lord. Even though this was misguided zeal, it was impressive courage—a Roman cohort was composed of 800 men! Earlier, when the Lord warned Peter of his impending denial of Him, Peter challenged the Son of God Himself, declaring, **"Even if I have to die with You, I will not deny You"** (Matt. 26:35). Peter considered himself to be a man of courage and was willing to die for the Lord. He just did not know where the courage came from. The Lord did not cause Peter to fall that night; He just removed the grace on which he was standing. Then the fearless man who had charged a Roman cohort could not even stand before a servant girl (see Matt. 26:69-75).

None of us can stand at any moment except by the grace of God. This is more than a cliché—it is a basic biblical truth. When we condemn others who are having problems, we are putting ourselves in jeopardy of falling to the same sins. That is why Paul warned us: **"Brethren, even if anyone is caught in any trespass, you who are spiritual, restore such a one in a spirit of gentleness; each one looking to yourself, so that you too will not be tempted"** (Gal. 6:1).

Whom Are We Criticizing?

When we criticize another Christian, we are actually saying that God's workmanship does not meet up to our standards—that we could do it better. When we criticize someone else's children, who takes offense? The parents! This is no less true of God. When we judge one of His people, we are judging Him. When we judge one of His leaders, we are actually judging *His* leadership. We are saying that He does not know what He is doing with the leadership that He is providing.

Such grumbling and complaining is the same problem that kept the first generation of the children of Israel from possessing their

Promised Land. Their grumbling caused them to spend their entire lives wandering in dry places, and this is still the chief reason why so many Christians do not walk in the promises of God. We have been warned:

> **Do not speak against one another, brethren. He who speaks against a brother or judges his brother, speaks against the law and judges the law; but if you judge the law, you are not a doer of the law but a judge of it. There is only one Lawgiver and Judge, the One who is able to save and to destroy** [when we judge the law, we judge the Lawgiver]**; but who are you who judge your neighbor** (James 4:11-12).

When we point the finger to criticize, we yoke ourselves.

> **Judge not, that you be not be judged. For with what judgment you judge, you will be judged; and with the measure you use, it will be measured back to you** (Matthew 7:1-2 NKJV).

The text in Isaiah 58 implies that the primary reason for the darkness, lack of healing, unanswered prayer, and lack of the glory of God, is our own critical spirit, which is called **"the pointing of the finger and speaking wickedness."** In the many people I have met who had exceptional mantles of spiritual authority, but who were lacking in spiritual fruit, this characteristic always seemed prevalent. They had judged and criticized the ministries of others who were gaining influence and had thereby disqualified themselves from the grace of God in that area. Our criticisms will bring us to poverty. **"Death and life are in the power of the tongue, and those who love it will eat its fruit"** (Prov. 18:21).

As Solomon observed:

> **But the path of the just is like the shining sun, that shines ever brighter unto the perfect day. The way of the wicked**

is like darkness; they do not know what makes them stumble (Proverbs 4:18-19 NKJV).

If we are walking in righteousness, we walk in increasing light. On the other hand, those who stumble around in the dark seldom know the reason for that darkness. Otherwise they would not be living in it. The critical person is usually critical of everyone but himself, and therefore, he cannot see his own problems. The Lord stated that such a person is so busy looking for specks in the eyes of his brothers that he cannot see the big log in his own eye, which is the reason for his blindness (see Matt. 7:1-5).

Stumbling Blocks

The Lord indicated that the last thing we should ever want to be is a stumbling block. He said that it would be better for us not to have been born than to cause even one of His little ones to stumble. In that same conversation (see Matt. 18), He gave clear instructions about how we are to deal with a brother or sister who is in sin—so that we will not become a stumbling block.

First, we must go to the person in private. If he rejects our counsel, we should go to him again with another brother. Only after he rejects the second counsel should we ever go before the rest of the church with the issue. If we do not follow this pattern, we will be in jeopardy of suffering a fate worse than the person who is in sin—becoming a stumbling block (see Matt. 18:15-17).

This tendency toward unrighteous judgment in the Church is possibly why many will come to the Lord on Judgment Day, having done many great things in His name, but will still hear those terrible words: **"Depart from Me, you who practice lawlessness"** (Matt. 7:23). By the Lord's own teachings, it would be difficult to overstate the importance of this terrible sin of unrighteous judgment.

I have heard numerous excuses for not following the Matthew 18 pattern for dealing with sin, such as: "I knew they would not listen to me," or "If he has a public ministry, we have a right to expose him publicly." However, the Lord did not say that we only had to comply with His instructions when we knew people would listen to us. He obviously implied that at least some would not hear, which is why there are the subsequent steps.

As far as the public ministry excuse goes, this is also flawed logic, because every ministry is public, at least to some degree. Who determines the degree to which it has become so public that it frees us from compliance with God's Word? The Lord gave no such conditions. Those who take such liberties with the clear commandments given by Jesus Himself are by this logic claiming to have authority to add to the Word of God.

If we believe a man with a large ministry is in sin and if we are not able to persuade him with our discernment, then we must not be the one to execute the judgment. Do not accuse but intercede! The Lord is able to judge His own house, and He is able to make a way for us if we are the ones He wants to use. If He does not make a way for us, we must trust Him to do it in His own time. Again, this is to protect us from coming under a judgment that is more severe than the brother who is in sin faces.

If we have not followed the Lord's prescribed manner for dealing with a brother who is in sin, we have no right to talk about it to anyone else, much less to go public with it. It should not even be shared to get another's opinion on the matter. What we may call "getting someone else's opinion," God usually calls gossip. He is not fooled, and we will pay the price for such indiscretions. Even if we follow all of the steps in Matthew 18, determining that we should bring an issue before the church, our goal must always be to save the brother from his sin, not to expose him.

Chapter Six

LOVE AND VISION

In light of the last chapter's discussion, we should not become petty with the challenges of presumed sins in a brother's life because **"...love covers a multitude of sins"** (1 Pet. 4:8). The majority of us still have a few hundred things wrong with us. The Lord usually is dealing with one or two of them at a time because that is all we can take. One of satan's strategies is to distract us into trying to deal with the other 300 problems simultaneously, resulting in frustration and defeat. Matthew 18 was not given for our use as a club to beat up on each other or even given as permission to let a brother know how he offended us. If we have love, we will cover most of those sins, unless they are bringing unnecessary injury to our brother. We must use this Scripture and indeed all Scripture in love, not out of self-preservation or retaliation.

Of course, the Lord Jesus Himself is our perfect model. When He corrected the seven churches in Revelation, He gave us an example for bringing correction to the Church. He first praised each church and highlighted what they were doing right. He then straightforwardly addressed their problems. Incredibly, He even gave Jezebel time to repent. He then gave each church a wonderful promise of reward for overcoming their problems. The Lord never changes. When He brings correction today, it always comes wrapped in encouragement, hope, and promises.

The "accuser of the brethren" is also trying to bring correction to the Church. However, his methods and goals are obviously quite different. Jesus encourages and gives hope; satan condemns and imparts hopelessness. Jesus builds us up, so we can handle the correction; satan tears us down, trying to get us to quit. Jesus loves us and wants to lift us up. Satan's goal is always destruction.

Discernment

We must walk in discernment, as Paul declared, **"...Do you not judge those who are within the church"** (1 Cor. 5:12). However, we must be careful to note that criticism can be rooted in true discernment, so those we criticize may be in error. For example, many who have criticized the way others raised money through manipulation, hype, and sometimes outright deception, were accurate in their discernment. The issue is how we deal with what we discern—are we going to use it to accuse or to intercede? Which ministry are we a part of—the enemy's accusation or the Lord's intercession? How we deal with discernment can determine the outcome of our own spiritual lives.

> **A worthless person, a wicked man, walks with a perverse mouth; He winks with his eyes, he shuffles his feet, he points with his fingers; Perversity is in his heart, he devises evil continually, he sows discord. Therefore his calamity shall come suddenly; suddenly he shall be broken without remedy** (Proverbs 6:12-15 NKJV).

Much of what has been paraded as discernment is nothing less than suspicion—a pseudo-spiritual disguise used to mask territorial preservation. Regardless of whether we have the spiritual gift of discernment or not, we have clear guidelines in the Book of James for discerning the source of wisdom. Had we heeded those guidelines, it could have preserved the Church from some of our most humiliating failures:

> **Who is wise and understanding among you? Let him show by good conduct that his works are done in the meekness of wisdom. But if you have bitter envy and self-seeking**

in your hearts, do not boast and lie against the truth. This wisdom does not descend from above, but is earthly, sensual, demonic. For where envy and self-seeking exist, confusion and every evil thing are there. But the wisdom that is from above is first pure, then peaceable, gentle, willing to yield, full of mercy and good fruits, without partiality and without hypocrisy. Now the fruit of righteousness is sown in peace by those who make peace (James 3:13-18 NKJV).

We are saved by grace, and we will need all the grace we can get to make it through this life. If we want to receive more grace, we must give more grace, for we reap what we sow (see Gal. 6:7). If we expect to receive mercy, we must start sowing mercy. Most of us will need all the mercy we can get. The last thing we want to do is come before the Lord with our brother's blood on our hands, just as He warned:

You have heard that it was said to those of old, "You shall not murder, and whoever murders will be in danger of the judgment." But I say to you that whoever is angry with his brother without a cause shall be in danger of the judgment. And whoever says to his brother, "Raca!" [empty head] shall be in danger of the council. But whoever says, "You fool!" shall be in danger of hell fire. Therefore if you bring your gift to the altar, and there remember that your brother has something against you, leave your gift there before the altar, and go your way. First be reconciled to your brother, and then come and offer your gift. Agree with your adversary quickly, while you are on the way with him, lest your adversary deliver you to the judge, the judge hand you over to the officer, and you be thrown into prison [bondage]. Assuredly, I say to you, you will by no means get out of there till you have paid the last penny (Matthew 5:21-26 NKJV).

By this warning, it is clear that, if we have been guilty of slandering a brother, we should forget about our offerings to the Lord until we have been reconciled to our brother. He links slandering and offerings together because we think that our sacrifices and offerings can compensate for such sins, but they never will. We will stay locked in the prisons we have built for ourselves with our judgments until we have paid the last cent or until we are reconciled to the brother that we slandered.

The Lord said that, when He returned, He would judge between the sheep and the goats (see Matt. 25:31-46). Those who are judged as sheep will inherit the Kingdom and eternal life. Those who are designated goats will be sent to eternal judgment. The separation will be determined by how each group has treated the Lord, which will be determined by how they have treated His people.

> **If someone says, "I love God," and hates his brother, he is a liar; for the one who does not love his brother whom he has seen, cannot love God whom he has not seen** (1 John 4:20).

> **Everyone who hates his brother is a murderer; and you know that no murderer has eternal life abiding in him. We know love by this, that He laid down His life for us; and we ought to lay down our lives for the brethren** (1 John 3:15-16).

If we really have Christ's Spirit, we will also possess His nature. How many of us, knowing that our best friends, who we had poured our lives into for more than three years, were about to desert us, denying that they ever knew us, would have **"earnestly desired"** to have one last meal with them? (See Luke 22:15.) Our Lord's love for His disciples was never conditional upon their doing right. Even though He knew they were about to desert Him and deny Him, He loved them to the end and even gave His life for them. When He saw our sins, He did not criticize us; He laid down His life for us. He has commanded us to love with that same love.

Winning the War Between Generations

One of the great tragedies of Church history has been the way leaders of each move of God have become opposers and persecutors of succeeding moves. To date, this trend has not failed. The Lord uses this to help purify and work humility into those He is about to release with increasing power and authority, but this is still a great tragedy. Numerous leaders have spent their lives serving faithfully only to finish as vessels for the accuser, who made them a stumbling block for the next move.

What is it that causes leaders of one move to become opposers of the next move? Several factors are involved, which we must understand and be delivered of, or we will find ourselves guilty of the same actions. We might think and say we would never do such things, but that is what previous church leaders thought and said as well. **"Therefore let him who thinks he stands take heed that he does not fall"** (1 Cor. 10:12). The pride that causes us to assume that we will not do such a thing is one of the factors that leads us to do it.

This problem actually precedes Church history and goes all the way back to the very first two brothers born into this world. John observed why the older could not bear the younger:

> **For this is the message which you have heard from the beginning, that we should love one another; not as Cain, who was of the evil one and slew his brother. And for what reason did he slay him? Because his deeds were evil, and his brother's were righteous** (1 John 3:11-12).

Each new move of the Holy Spirit has resulted in the restoration of more light to the Church. This light is not new truth but truth that was lost to the Church through the Dark Ages of her history. Regardless of what we call our opposition, the basic reason for most of it is jealousy. Some in leadership, or those who have been faithful to the light that they have had for a time, have difficulty believing that anyone is more worthy or that the Lord would use anyone but them for further restoration of His truth and purposes.

Only one remedy will keep leaders from ultimately falling to this terrible trap—seeking the humility and nature of John the Baptist. He was one of the greatest types of true spiritual ministry. His whole purpose in life was to prepare the way for Jesus, to point to Him, then to decrease as the greater One increased (see John 3:30). John's joy was to see the One who followed him going further than he went.

On the other hand, if we are part of an emerging generation, we must realize that the pride of thinking we are better than those who went before us can disqualify us from going any further ourselves. The only commandment with a promise is that which commands us to honor our fathers and mothers, referring to both our natural and spiritual fathers and mothers. The promise is that you will **"remain long in the land which the Lord has given you"** (Exod. 20:12). Our spiritual longevity is directly related to this one issue.

Many years ago, when I inquired of the Lord how to honor my spiritual fathers and mothers, the Lord replied that, just as Israel considered it an honor to drink from the wells that their ancestors had dug, I could also honor my spiritual fathers and mothers by drinking from their spiritual wells. I began to do this and have found treasures of wisdom and knowledge that are beyond earthly value.

This is also one of the many ways that the Lord has saved the best wine for last. For example, many of the books and messages given to us by our spiritual fathers and mothers contain an entire lifetime of experience and wisdom that we can receive in a couple of hours or days. I spent nearly 30 years accumulating the knowledge and understanding condensed into this book, which you can read in a few hours. How will we ever be able to thank the Lord enough for letting us live in these times?

Scientists today would be very limited in developing technology if they had to begin by reinventing the wheel and taking every step over themselves from that point on. We would still be living in the Stone Age. The increase of knowledge that has created such technological advancement is mirrored by a similar spiritual increase of knowledge that is preparing to release a generation into realms of the Spirit that the Lord promised would enable us to do things that He did and even greater things. We must not miss this unprecedented opportunity. None of it would be possible without what Jesus and those who have gone before us did. To fail to honor them is to sever ourselves from the faith and humility that enables us to receive it.

Chapter Seven

THE HEART OF THE FREEDOM FIGHTER

In order for the Church to advance, future spiritual leaders must become "spiritual eunuchs." An eunuch's whole purpose was to prepare the bride for the king. It was not possible for the eunuch to desire the bride, but his joy was wrapped up in his king's joy. When we use the ministry in order to build a reputation for ourselves or to find those who will serve us, we will not be of the same authority as Christ. Paul exhorted us:

> **Do nothing from selfishness or empty conceit, but with humility of mind regard one another as more important than yourselves; do not merely look out for your own personal interests, but also for the interests of others. Have this attitude in yourselves which was also in Christ Jesus, who, although He existed in the form of God, did not regard equality with God a thing to be grasped, but emptied Himself, taking the form of a bond-servant, and being made in the likeness of men. Being found in appearance as a man, He humbled Himself by becoming obedient to the point of death, even death on a cross. For this reason also, God highly exalted Him, and bestowed on Him the name which is above every name** (Philippians 2:3-9).

This Scripture is the pattern that Jesus set for everyone who would follow Him in leadership. Humility comes before authority and position. He said in Luke 14:11: **"For everyone who exalts himself**

will be humbled, and he who humbles himself will be exalted." A key word here is *everyone.* James added, **"Humble yourselves in the presence of the Lord, and He will exalt you"** (James 4:10). Peter stated, **"Therefore humble yourselves under the mighty hand of God, that He may exalt you at the proper time"** (1 Pet. 5:6). In all of these texts, we see that it is our job to humble ourselves, and it is the Lord's job to do the exalting. It is clear that, if we try to do His job, He will do our job, and He can do either one of them much better than we can.

The evil spirits of self-promotion and territorial preservation have done much damage to the Church. They have caused many potentially great leaders to be disqualified from receiving further anointing and authority. The influence we gain by our own self-promotion or manipulation will become a stumbling block that keeps us from attaining positions that God would have otherwise given to us.

It has not always been the older generation of leaders that were the stumbling block for the new. The new generation can be just as guilty of causing the previous one to stumble. The very arrogance of presuming that we are the new generation reveals a pride that God has to resist. This presumption is a humiliating slap in the face to men and women who have given their lives to faithfully serving the Lord and His people.

Jesus did not ridicule John the Baptist for being a part of the old order—He honored him. Jesus even submitted Himself to John's ministry. This submission did not mean that He allowed John to control Him; instead, He acknowledged John and esteemed him and his work.

Later, when Jesus was asked the source of His authority, he pointed to John and asked His inquisitors if they knew from where John's baptism came. The answer to His question was the answer to their question (see Matt. 21:23-27). John was the last of an order—he was there to represent all of those who had prophesied the coming Messiah from the very beginning. John was their representative, acknowledging Jesus as the One of whom they all had spoken—that

He was indeed the Lamb of God. Jesus acknowledged the baptism of those who had gone before Him as the credentials of His authority.

Those of the new generation must likewise submit to the ministry of those who have gone before them if they are to fulfill all righteousness. We are presently in the midst of seeing a new spiritual generation emerge. It is also apparent that the previous movements are beginning to decrease as the new order emerges. However, it is crucial that the leaders of the new order honor those who went before them, or they will be in jeopardy of disqualifying themselves from advancing in the Kingdom. The arrogance of the new order can be just as much of an affront to the Spirit of God as that of the old who resist God in the new things He begins to do.

Why the Abused Become the Abusers

As I previously mentioned when discussing the "tyranny of the familiar," one of the baffling questions is why people get trapped in cycles of oppression and bondage and refuse to go free, even when they are able to. Many abused children who swear that they will never grow up like their parents will inevitably grow up to be abusers. Why is it that many accused saints grow up to become accusers? The answer is the same for both. Abused children usually grow up determined not to be like their parents; thus they become reactionary, which does not lead to grace, but can actually nurture bitterness. This ultimately can result in them becoming just like their parents. Only humility and forgiveness can ever break that cycle.

The sins of the parents will become the sins of the children until we receive the grace of the cross. Because God gives grace to the humble, we must understand that we will take on the sins of our parents without His help. That is one reason why many of the great leaders in Scripture prayed to be forgiven for the sins of their fathers.

Elijah Must Come

There will be a spiritual generation that will be persecuted just as every one before it; however, they will not go on to persecute the next generation. This movement will not be subject to the "pride of generations," assuming that all things will be concluded with them. Those in this generation will find the grace of the cross and will forgive from the heart those who mistreat them. They will perceive and even have hope that their children, spiritual and natural, may go further in Christ than they did, and they will rejoice in it. They will give their lives to make the way of the next generation as smooth as possible, and then they will rejoice to decrease as that generation arises. This will be the generation of the spirit of Elijah who will return the hearts of the fathers to the children, and the hearts of the children to the fathers (see Mal. 4:6).

Our ability to be the generation that prepares the way for the Lord and His ultimate purposes will be determined by the ministry we become a part of—accusation or intercession. Let us now remove the terrible yoke of "pointing the finger" from our midst and begin turning our criticisms into intercession.

> **Then your light will break out like the dawn, and your recovery will speedily spring forth; and your righteousness will go before you; the glory of the Lord will be your rear guard. Then you will call, and the Lord will answer; you will cry, and He will say, "Here I am." If you remove the yoke from your midst, the pointing of the finger and speaking wickedness…. And the Lord will continually guide you, and satisfy your desire in scorched places, and give strength to your bones; and you will be like a watered garden, and like a spring of water whose waters do not fail. Those from among you will rebuild the ancient ruins; you will raise up the age-old foundations; and you will be called the repairer of the breach, the restorer of the streets in which to dwell** (Isaiah 58:8-9;11-12).

According to this text, the **"pointing of the finger,"** or that critical spirit, is the reason why there is so little light, healing, answered prayer, or the glory of the Lord revealed. Turning our criticisms into intercession can be the one thing that most radically changes the life, power, and glory that we experience in the Lord. It can do it for the Church and for us as individuals. If we do this, we will be those who restore the age-old foundations, repair the breach between God and humankind, and therefore, between people and other people. Then the glory will come. All we are doing is trading our bitterness for glory. Isn't it time to do this?

Because love covers a multitude of sins, let us determine that we are going to grow in love by covering other people's sins against us. Start with the person who irritates you the most, whether it is your spouse, boss, pastor, etc. Now consider what it is they do that irritates you the most. This is your greatest opportunity to grow in love. Determine that you are going to cover that which irritates you and start praying for the Lord to bless that person. Then start using other things that irritate you as a call to grow in love. If you do this, your life will radically change and so will the lives of all who are close to you.

THE STRONGHOLD
OF WITCHCRAFT

Chapter Eight

UNDERSTANDING WITCHCRAFT

The practice of witchcraft has dramatically increased throughout the world in recent years. One of the expressed goals of many involved in this movement is to destroy Christianity. Many Christians are presently suffering some form of attack from those who practice witchcraft. Discerning the nature of these attacks and knowing how to overcome them is becoming crucial for all believers. The only way that Christians can be defeated is through our own ignorance or complacency. As we maintain our position in Christ, taking on the full armor of God and remaining vigilant, we will not only stand but will prevail against any attack from hell.

What Is Witchcraft?

Witchcraft is counterfeit spiritual authority; it is using a spirit other than the Holy Spirit to dominate, manipulate, or control others.

In Galatians 5:20, the apostle Paul named witchcraft, or **"sorcery,"** as one of the deeds of the flesh. Though witchcraft has its origin in the carnal nature of man, it usually degenerates quickly into demonic power. Using emotional pressure to manipulate others is a basic form of witchcraft. Using hype or soul power to enlist service, even for the work of God, is witchcraft. When businessmen scheme to find pressure points while pursuing a deal, it can also be considered witchcraft. Many of the manipulative tactics promoted as sales techniques in marketing are basic forms of witchcraft.

The primary defense against counterfeit spiritual authority is to walk in true spiritual authority. Establishing our lives on truth and trusting in the Lord to accomplish what concerns us are essential keys to becoming free from the influence and pressure of witchcraft.

It is written that Jesus is seated upon the throne of David (see Isa. 9:1-7). This indicates that David established a position of true spiritual authority that would ultimately be manifested in the Kingdom of God. David did for spiritual authority what Abraham did for faith.

How did David establish a seat of true authority? Basically, he refused to take authority or seek influence for himself but completely trusted in God to establish him in the position that He had ordained for him. David did not lift his own hand to seek recognition or influence, and neither should we if we want to walk in true spiritual authority rather than mere human political power.

Any authority or influence that we gain by our own manipulation or self-promotion will become a stumbling block to us and will hinder our ability to receive true authority from God. If we want to walk in true spiritual authority like David, we will have to utterly trust in the Lord to establish us in it in His time. As Peter exhorted, **"Therefore humble yourselves under the mighty hand of God, that He may exalt you at the proper time"** (1 Pet. 5:6).

Someone once made the observation that "premature responsibility breeds superficiality." Possibly nothing is more devastating to our calling and potential for walking in true ministry than seeking influence or authority prematurely.

When the Lord promotes, He also supplies the grace and wisdom to carry the authority. No greater security is available than knowing that God is the One who has established our ministry. Few things can breed insecurity faster than trying to maintain a position that we have gained by our own promotion or manipulation. This is the root of most of the territorial preservation and division that exist in the Body of Christ.

Being established in true spiritual authority is a fortress that simply cannot be penetrated by the enemy. **"The God of peace will soon crush Satan under your feet..."** (Rom. 16:20). When we know that we have been given our authority and have been established in our position by God, we have a peace that will utterly crush the enemy's attacks against us.

In contrast, when we establish ourselves in a position of authority, we will have little peace. The more our illegally gained influence increases, the more striving and manipulating it will take to hold it together. Anything that we do through manipulation, hype, or soul power, regardless of seemingly noble goals, is doomed to ultimate failure.

Therefore, the first principle in being delivered from the influence of witchcraft is to repent of all the ways that we ourselves have used it in our own lives and ministries. Satan cannot cast out satan. Witchcraft, in even its most evil and diabolical forms such as black magic, will have an open door into our lives if we ourselves are using manipulation to control others or gain position.

Although we may try to justify using such devices in order to build the Church, God is not fooled and neither is the enemy. What God is building is not raised up by might nor by power but by His Spirit (see Zech. 4:6). Whatever we build by any other means is an affront to the cross and will ultimately oppose that which the Spirit is doing. The flesh wars against the Spirit, regardless of how good we try to make the flesh look.

Spiritual Maturity

One of the primary ways that the Lord works in our lives to help us overcome our tendency to use manipulative tactics is by allowing us to endure rejection. Rejection is the one thing we hate the most, and it even seems that the Lord's greatest trial on the cross was the rejection He suffered when the Father turned away from Him. Because rejection can be such a difficult trial, it can also be a great opportunity to be delivered from the fear of man and the fear of rejection, which can devastate any life or ministry.

Almost everyone in ministry must endure considerable rejection and misunderstanding. Learning to overcome rejection, by forgiving and praying for our persecutors just as the Lord did, is essential if we are to walk in the Spirit and exercise true spiritual authority. If we are to accomplish the purposes of God, we must come to the level of maturity where, **"the love of Christ controls us"** (2 Cor. 5:14). Love does not take into account the wrongs we have suffered and is not motivated by rejection, which drives us to retaliate or try to prove ourselves. Such reactions are the first step in a fall from true authority. As the Lord Jesus stated:

> **He who speaks from himself seeks his own glory** [literally "recognition"]**; but He who is seeking the glory** [recognition] **of the One who sent Him, He is true, and there is no unrighteousness in Him** (John 7:18).

There are few things that will more quickly destroy our ability to walk in true spiritual authority than self-seeking, self-promotion, or self-preservation. On the other hand, learning to deal with rejection is mandatory if we are to walk in a true ministry. Rejection provides an opportunity for us to grow in grace and to die a little more to ambition, pride, and other motives that so quickly color our revelation. If we embrace rejection as a discipline of the Lord, we will grow in grace and love. If we rebel against this discipline, we may enter into witchcraft.

The Fear of Man Leads to Witchcraft

King Saul is a good example of how a man with a true commission from God can fall into this counterfeit spiritual authority. When he was commanded to wait for Samuel before offering the sacrifice, he succumbed to pressure and offered it prematurely, saying, **"...I saw that the people were scattering from me...and that the Philistines were assembling..."** (1 Sam. 13:11). This is the same point where most fall from true authority—when they begin to fear the people or the circumstances more than they fear God. When we start to fear the people leaving more than we fear God leaving, we will have departed from true faith.

Because witchcraft is basically rooted in the fear of man, and **"the fear of man brings a snare..."** (Prov. 29:25), those who operate in witchcraft are trapped because fear has snared them. The bigger the project or ministry that we have built with hype, manipulation, or control spirits, the more we will fear anyone or anything that we cannot manipulate or control. Those who are caught in this deadly trap will fear those who walk in the true anointing and authority, because those who walk in true spiritual authority are the least affected by manipulation or the spirit of control.

Saul became enraged at David and was consumed with destroying him, even though David was at the time but **"a single flea"** (1 Sam. 24:14). As the manipulation and control spirits increase their dominion, so will the paranoia of those who are trapped within their grasp. Such people will become irrationally consumed by an attempt to drive out or destroy anyone who threatens their control.

Those who receive their authority, recognition, or security from people, like Saul, will end up in the witch's house. Samuel warned Saul that **"rebellion is as the sin of witchcraft"** (1 Sam. 15:23 NKJV). When one in spiritual authority rebels against the Holy Spirit, the void will be filled by the counterfeit spiritual authority of witchcraft. This may begin as a simple reliance upon hype and soul power, but without repentance, it can end up in the most diabolical forms of presumption and rebellion, as we see in the case of King Saul. Persecuting those who were faithful to the Lord, Saul killed the true priests and spent one of his last nights in the house of a witch as the natural conclusion to the direction his life had taken (see 1 Sam. 22:28).

Spiritual authority is a dangerous occupation. If we are wise, like David, we will not seek a position of authority, and we will not even take one which is offered until we are certain that the Lord is the one giving it. Satan tempts everyone called by God with the same temptation he offered to Jesus—if we will bow down to him and his ways, he will give us authority over kingdoms (see Matt. 4:8-10). God has called us to rule over kingdoms too, but His way leads to the cross. The authority He offers us can only be attained if we become servants of all (see Mark 9:35). Satan's temptation is to offer the quick and easy path to the same place to which God has in fact called us.

Presumption Kills

One of the most frequent phrases attributed to David's life was, **"David inquired of the Lord..."** (1 Sam. 30:8). On the few occasions when David made major decisions without inquiring of the Lord, the consequences were devastating. The higher the position of authority, the more dangerous it is and the more people are affected by even seemingly insignificant decisions. True spiritual authority is not an honor to be sought; it is a burden to be carried. Many who seek authority and influence do not know what they are asking for. Immaturity can be our doom if authority is given to us before our time.

Even though David lived a thousand years before the age of grace, he knew the Lord's grace and lived by it. Yet he still made mistakes that cost thousands of lives. Solomon had observed God's grace in his father's life, which was probably what caused him to desire wisdom to rule over God's people above all else. Anyone called to a position of leadership in the Church must have the same devotion. Even if we are not in a position of spiritual authority, presumption can kill us. If we are in a position of authority, presumption will almost certainly lead to our fall and can lead to the fall of many others as well.

The gift of a word of knowledge can be a remarkable demonstration of power, but those who are called to walk in spiritual authority would do well to seek words of wisdom—even more than words of knowledge. We need demonstrations of power and words of knowledge to accomplish the work of the Lord, but it is essential that we also have the wisdom to use them properly.

Humility Is a Safety Net

Those who attain prominence before humility will almost certainly fall. If we have wisdom, we will seek humility before position. True authority operates on the grace of God, and the more authority we walk in, the more grace we will need. *We only have true spiritual authority to the degree that the King lives within us.* True spiritual authority is not position; it is grace. Counterfeit spiritual authority stands on its position instead of grace. Jesus is the highest spiritual authority, and He used His position to lay down His life. He commanded those who would come after Him to take up their crosses and do the same (see Matt. 16:24).

Protection From Charismatic Witchcraft

Those in leadership must not only be wary of using witchcraft, they must also be aware that they will be the primary target of those who do. Witchcraft is an enemy that we must guard against from within and without. It is just as subtle when it attacks from without as when it takes ground from within. This form of sorcery is seldom what we call black magic, but is usually a form of "white witchcraft." Those who practice it are often well-meaning people who do not have the confidence to be straightforward and have therefore fallen to subtle forms of manipulation to gain influence.

One prominent form of white witchcraft, which is common in the Church, can be described as "charismatic witchcraft." This has nothing to do with the Charismatic Movement, but is a pseudo-spirituality. It often uses this guise to gain influence or control of others or situations. It is a source of many false prophecies, dreams, and visions, which can ultimately destroy or neutralize a church or bring the leadership to the point where they overreact so as to despise prophecy altogether. Those using this form of witchcraft will usually think that they have the mind of the Lord, which gives them the greater authority. They will therefore conclude that the leadership, or anyone else who contradicts them, is in rebellion.

Jezebel

Jezebel is an archetype of witchcraft in Scripture. She used her power to control her husband, Ahab, the king, and therefore, she had the real authority over Israel. She was also able to bring such depression upon Elijah that he sought death over life, even after his greatest spiritual victory (see 1 Kings 19:1-4). There is power in witchcraft. Those who are ignorant of it or who presumptuously disregard its potential to affect them are very often brought down by it. Many churches, ministries, movements, and even revivals have been stopped or destroyed by this evil. All who walk in true spiritual authority must understand it, or it will become a significant threat to all that they accomplish.

Jezebel may have easily overpowered Ahab, but Elijah was certainly no wimp. He single-handedly confronted and destroyed more than 800 false prophets in one of the greatest demonstrations of God's power over evil in all of history. Yet immediately after this, one woman, operating in the power of witchcraft, was able to send the great prophet fleeing in discouragement. This story reveals the kind of power to discourage that witchcraft can have on anyone.

How can this happen? Compared to the power of God, all the power of the evil one would not even register on the scale! The newest babe in Christ has more power dwelling in him than all the antichrists put together. How is it that we can still be overcome by evil? It is because satan does not confront God's people with power; *he distracts and seduces them with deception.*

Compared to the 800 false prophets, who was this one woman to challenge Elijah? Certainly he could have destroyed her power more easily than he had destroyed the power of the false prophets. It was not rational for Elijah to have become so discouraged because of Jezebel's threat, but that is precisely the point. This attack did not come through reasoning; it was a spiritual attack. Reasoning usually has little to do with the power of witchcraft.

Jezebel slammed Elijah immediately after his greatest victory, and it overpowered him. We will often be most vulnerable to this kind of an attack after a great victory because it is then that we tend to drop our guard and become most open to pride. Our first defense against the attacks of the enemy through witchcraft, or any other tactic, should be to maintain the humility of knowing that we are standing only by God's grace. Pride leaves a breach in our armor that the enemy can easily penetrate.

Chapter Nine

THE STINGS OF WITCHCRAFT

The attacks of witchcraft usually come in a series of stings. The successive stings are meant to hit the very places where we have been weakened by the previous stings. In this way they build upon each other until the cumulative effect overwhelms the target. The stings of witchcraft usually come in the following order:

1. Discouragement
2. Confusion
3. Depression
4. Loss of Vision
5. Disorientation
6. Withdrawal
7. Despair
8. Defeat

This process can happen quickly, as it did with Elijah, but it usually works more slowly, which makes it even more difficult to discern. However, if we know the enemy's schemes, we will not continue to be subject to them. When these symptoms begin to make inroads into our lives, we must identify them and resist the enemy until he flees. If we do not resist him, we will be the ones fleeing just like Elijah.

The source of witchcraft used against us may not always be through the obvious satanic cults or New Age operatives. It can come from well-meaning, though deceived, Christians. These are the ones who start praying against leaders instead of for them. These misguided prayers have power because whatever is released on earth is released in Heaven, and whatever is bound on earth is bound in Heaven (see Matt. 16:19). If intercession is motivated by a spirit of control or manipulation, it is witchcraft and can have the same devastating power as black magic.

Other sources of charismatic witchcraft can be such things as gossip, political maneuvering, and jealousy, and they can have an effect on us whether we allow ourselves to be manipulated by them or not. For example, consider the result if we refuse to be manipulated by someone who has a control spirit but allow ourselves to become resentful or bitter toward that person. In such a case, the enemy has still caused us to fall. The discouragement, disorientation, and depression will come upon us just as surely as if we had submitted to the control spirit.

We are defeated by the enemy when he can get us to respond in any spirit other than the Holy Spirit, whose fruit is love, joy, peace, and so forth (see Gal. 5:22-23). The enemy's strategy is to cause us to depart from the fruit of the Holy Spirit and try to combat him in our own strength. Remember that satan cannot cast out satan, and resentment will never cast out Jezebel—it will only increase her power.

Therefore, the basic strategy we must use to begin freeing ourselves from the power of witchcraft is to *bless those who curse us* (see Rom. 12:14). This does not mean that we bless their works but that we pray for them and not against them. If the enemy can get us to retaliate, he will then have succeeded in causing us to use the same spirit, and we will have multiplied the very evil we were trying to cast out.

We are not warring against flesh and blood, and the weapons of our warfare are not carnal but spiritual (see Eph. 6:12; 2 Cor. 10:3-5). When we begin to pray blessings upon the people who are attacking us, then the evil power of control and manipulation is broken over both them and us. We must not return evil for evil; we must *overcome evil with good* (see Rom. 12:21).

Discerning the Stings of Witchcraft

Sting 1—Discouragement

Everyone gets discouraged at times, and it can be for many different reasons. Discouragement is not always the result of witchcraft being used against us. However, if we become subject to increasing discouragement for no apparent reason, witchcraft should be considered as a possible source.

When difficulties seem insurmountable and you want to give up, even though matters are not any worse than usual, you are probably coming under spiritual attack. The enemy's attempt to afflict you with discouragement is meant to weaken you for the next level of attack, which is:

Sting 2—Confusion

Again, we must look for a general and increasing "spirit of confusion" for which there is no apparent reason. We begin to lose clarity about what we have been called to do, which of course will weaken our resolve. This confusion is meant to compound our discouragement, making us even weaker and more vulnerable to further attack, which will usually come in the form of:

Sting 3—Depression

Depression is a deeper problem than simple discouragement. It is an unshakable dread that comes as a result of the combined effect of discouragement and confusion, along with a general negligence in spiritual disciplines that has usually slipped in by this time. Depression will become an increasingly prevalent problem in the last days, and we must gain victory over it. If we do not, it will quickly lead to the next sting:

Sting 4—Loss of Vision

Loss of Vision is the goal of the previous stings, and it works to increase their effect. We begin to doubt that God has called us to the task in the first place. The only way we can sail through the storm of confusion is to hold our course, but we cannot hold our course if we do not know where we are going. We will not try to hold our course if we begin to think it was wrong for us to ever pursue our vision in the first place. Such a loss in vision will lead to our drifting in circles at the time when we most need to **"make straight paths for your feet"** (Heb. 12:13). This sets us up for the next level of assault:

Sting 5—Disorientation

The combined result of depression, confusion, and loss of vision is usually disorientation. By this time, not only have we forgotten the course we are supposed to be holding, but we have even lost our ability to read the compass. The Scriptures will no longer speak to us, and it is a struggle to trust the Lord's voice or receive much encouragement from even the most anointed teaching or preaching. This is the point of spiritual incapacitation, the inability to function, which results in:

Sting 6—Withdrawal

When disorientation sets in, it is tempting to withdraw or retreat from our purpose in the ministry, our fellowship with the rest of the Church, and often from our families and others we are close to. Withdrawal will result in:

Sting 7—Despair

Withdrawal from the battle leads quickly to hopelessness and despair. Without hope, we can easily be taken out by the enemy, either through temptation, sickness, or death. Science has proven that when hope is removed, even the most healthy person will quickly deteriorate and die. With hope, men and women have lived long past the point when a normal body would have quit. Despair will always lead to:

Sting 8—Defeat

The enemy's purpose is to weaken us so that we begin to fall further and further behind so that we can be more easily picked off. In

Scripture, the Amalekites typified satan and his hordes. It was the practice of the Amalekites to attack the weak and defenseless. As the camp of Israel crossed the wilderness, the Amalekites picked off the loners or stragglers who fell behind the rest of the camp.

Through witchcraft, the enemy seeks to weaken believers so that they will begin to fall behind the rest of the camp and become easy prey. Israel was warned that there would be perpetual war with the Amalekites. When Israel's kings were commanded to fight them, they were also commanded to utterly destroy them and not take any spoil. We have a perpetual war against satan, and we cannot take any prisoners. Neither can we use that which is his in the service of God.

King Saul disobeyed this command, keeping Agag, king of the Amalekites, alive and also keeping some of the spoil **"to sacrifice to the Lord"** (1 Sam. 15:15). This was a failure of the most foolish kind for one called to lead God's people. In those days, keeping a rival king alive after a battle was only done for one of two reasons: to make him an ally or a slave. Saul foolishly thought that he could make the one who personified satan himself into an ally or a slave.

It was no accident that it was an Amalekite who killed Saul and carried the news of Saul's death to David. This Amalekite thought that the news would be pleasing to David, but David was discerning and had him killed (see 2 Sam. 1:1-16). If we do not obey the Lord and utterly destroy the enemy we battle, he will eventually finish us off. There can be no alliance with the enemy. He and his hordes must utterly be destroyed. Let us not be foolish enough to think that we can use the enemy as our slave. In his guile, he will quickly turn the tables.

Witchcraft is being used against the Church. Many who have failed to recognize it have been defeated, losing their vision, their ministry, their families, and even their lives. This is not sensationalism; it is fact. Paul said that we do not wrestle against flesh and blood, but against principalities and powers (see Eph. 6:12). Wrestling is the closest form of combat. The enemy is going to fight, and he is going to wrestle with us. If we decide that we are just not going to fight, we will get pinned.

As Christians, we have no option as to whether or not we are going to do spiritual warfare—if we want to survive, we must fight. But how do we combat this witchcraft? We must first look at the basic principle of spiritual warfare required for every victory.

Chapter Ten

VICTORY OVER WITCHCRAFT

In Revelation 12:11, we see that the saints overcome satan by:

1. the blood of the Lamb,
2. the word of their testimony, and
3. they did not love their lives even when faced with death.

We overcome by the blood of the Lamb as we take our stand on what He has already accomplished for us by the cross. The victory has already been won and there is no way we can lose if we abide in Him.

The word of our testimony is the Scriptures. Every time the enemy challenged Jesus, He simply responded with Scripture, countering the enemy's temptation with God's truth (see Matt. 4:1-11). If the Word Himself took His stand on the written Word, how much more should we? The Word of God is **"...the sword of the Spirit..."** (Eph. 6:17). With the sword, we can deflect the blows from the enemy's deceptive words, as well as attack him. Of all the pieces of armor that we are commanded to use, the sword is the only offensive weapon (see Eph. 6:10-18).

That they **"...loved not their lives unto the death"** (Rev. 12:11 KJV), is the utter commitment to follow Him regardless of the price. We are called to take up our crosses daily, to do all things for the sake of the Gospel, and to no longer live for ourselves but for Him. To the degree that we remain in self-centeredness, we will be vulnerable to the enemy's attack. When we have reckoned ourselves dead to this world, as crucified with Christ, then the enemy no longer has any access to us because he has no more access to Him. What can be done to a dead person? It is impossible for the dead to be offended, to be tempted, to fear, to be depressed, or to be continually looking for the easy way out, because they have already paid the ultimate price.

All of these—the blood of the Lamb, the word of our testimony, and a commitment to lay down our lives—are required for spiritual victory. Anything less will fail to bring a complete victory. We may make occasional, halting advances, but we will sooner or later be pushed back. However, it is clear that, at the end of the age, an army of believers will be raised up who will not settle for occasional advances—they will have committed themselves to the fight and will not stop until they have the total victory. **"The earth is the Lord's, and all it contains..."** (Ps. 24:1). Until the earth has been completely recovered from the domain of satan, our fight is not over.

No one will fight to win if they do not believe victory is possible. Many teachings that declare the Church's defeat before Christ's return have been promulgated. Yet the whole prophetic testimony of Scripture is that the Lord, the Church, and the truth are going to prevail. Satan is indeed being cast down to the earth, bringing with him a time of trouble like the world has never known before—but we will still win!

Isaiah 14:16-17 says that when we see satan we are going to marvel at the pitiful nature of the one who caused so much trouble! He who lives within the very least of the saints is much greater than the combined power of all antichrists. These times are not to be feared—this will be our finest hour! As Isaiah 60:1-2 declares, when darkness covers the earth, the glory of the Lord will appear on His people. The darkness will make His glory upon us appear that much brighter. We must start fighting in order to win, giving no more ground to the enemy and taking back what he has usurped.

To effectively combat witchcraft, we must determine that we are going to resist satan until he flees from us. Our goal is more than just driving the enemy out of our own lives; we must also pursue him until he is driven out of others in whom he has established a stronghold. The following are some ways we can combat and overcome eight specific areas of satan's attack through witchcraft.

1. Overcoming Discouragement

Discouragement never comes from God. He is the author of faith and the source of hope which never disappoints. Although God disciplines us when we need it, He never does so by afflicting us with discouragement. When James describes the wisdom that comes from above, he does not list discouragement as one of the characteristics: **"But the wisdom from above is first pure, then peaceable, gentle, reasonable, full of mercy and good fruits, unwavering, without hypocrisy"** (James 3:17). Discouragement is the very opposite of love, joy, peace, and other attributes of the Holy Spirit's fruit (see Gal. 5:22-23).

We must learn to quickly and instinctively reject discouragement, giving it no place in our thoughts. We must tenaciously resist it, taking every thought captive to obey Christ (see 2 Cor. 10:5). Discouragement must never be allowed to dictate our course. *Faith* is the fruit of the Spirit and the shield of our armor that counters discouragement. If we begin to get discouraged, it is because we have dropped our shield. We need to pick it back up!

2. Overcoming Confusion

"God is not the author of confusion" (1 Cor. 14:33 KJV), so we can know for certain that, when confusion strikes, it is not coming from Him. In the military, confusion is one of the primary elements of battle that a soldier is trained to handle. Because nothing ever goes exactly as planned, there will rarely be a battle where there is not confusion; the same is true in spiritual warfare.

The disciplined soldier who understands this aspect of warfare learns to use the confusion to his own advantage. He does not let it increase his discouragement but begins to anticipate it, looking for an opportunity to gain an advantage over the enemy. We must learn to expect confusion as part of the battle and not be surprised or affected by it. Our resolve to stand and fight will quickly dispel this aspect of the attack.

3. Overcoming Depression

God told Cain the most effective remedy for depression:

Then the Lord said to Cain, "Why are you angry? And why has your countenance fallen [the ancient expression for depression]**? If you do well, will not your countenance be lifted up? And if you do not do well, sin is crouching at the door; and its desire is for you, but you must master it"** (Genesis 4:6-7).

Depression is usually the result of allowing discouragement and confusion to cause us to drift from our basic spiritual disciplines, such as reading the Word, praying, fellowshipping, and so forth. Practicing these disciplines again with resolve will almost always start to reverse the downward spiral.

4. Overcoming a Loss of Vision

This attack can also be turned to our advantage and used as an opportunity. When we begin to lose our vision, we must recommit ourselves to strengthening our vision more than ever. We need to sink our roots deeper and establish our purpose even more firmly upon the Word of God. When God begins to lead us into a purpose, we should record how He speaks to us. By searching all the Scriptures and reviewing the ways He has led us in the past, we will establish His leading even more firmly.

Above all, we must hold our course! We should not change our direction until we can clearly see the new course. In World War I, one of the most effective tactics of the enemy was to lay a smoke screen in front of Allied battleship convoys. As the convoy entered the smoke, visibility was lost. The ships would start turning at any perceived sound or whim, resulting in collisions that sunk more ships than enemy torpedoes did.

The Allies finally developed a simple strategy to thwart this tactic against their vision. When in the smoke, every ship was to hold its previous course without deviation. By doing so, they discovered that they would soon sail out of the other side into clear air. The same strategy will enable us to more quickly escape whatever is clouding our vision. When we lose our vision, we need to just hold our course and keep moving forward. We will soon break out into the clear.

5. Overcoming Disorientation

As an instrument flight instructor, the first thing I taught each student pilot was that he must not trust his feelings when experiencing restricted visibility while flying on instruments. If a pilot tries to fly by his feelings when in instrument conditions, he will quickly lose control of the plane. Even when flying perfectly straight and level through the clouds, it can begin to feel like the plane is turning. If the pilot reacts to this feeling, he will begin to turn in order to counteract this supposed drift, causing the plane to veer off course or possibly even turning the plane upside down.

In a test conducted by the FAA, a group of pilots without previous instrument training were flown into instrument conditions. Every one of them lost control of their planes because they relied on their feelings for guidance. The same is true of immature Christians who enter spiritual conditions of reduced visibility or "spiritual clouds." They usually try to rely on their feelings for guidance and, therefore, lose control.

The "instruments" we have been given to walk by are found in the Bible. We do not walk by feelings, but by faith in the sure testimony of the Word of God. The Word of God will keep us oriented and on course if we put our trust in it, even when our feelings may tell us to do otherwise.

6. Overcoming Withdrawal

In the Persian Gulf War, the majority of casualties were either reserves or civilians. The safest place to be in the war was on the front line. This has been true in most modern wars, and it is true in spiritual warfare as well.

When you are being pressed in a battle, you cannot call a time-out. On the frontline, we cannot ask the enemy to stop the battle because we have a headache or want to take a break. When we are on the frontline, we know the dangers, and we must not let our guard down.

All Christians are on the frontline every day whether they like it or not. Satan will not stop when we call a time-out. It is when we start to consider ourselves a "civilian," and not a soldier, that we will be the most vulnerable to his attack. Christians are never in the reserves. Of course, there are times of reprieve from conflict; seldom do battles continually rage along the entire front. However, when we know we are on the front, even our breaks are taken with vigilance, because we realize that a fresh attack can come at any time. Christians must never remove their spiritual armor or lose their vigilance.

In time of warfare, there are occasions when strategic retreat is necessary. At times, we may overcommit ourselves spiritually and must draw back—but that is not the same as withdrawing from the battle. Even when we overcommit ourselves, retreat should be a last resort because an army in retreat is in its most vulnerable condition. If at all possible, we should at least try to hold our ground until our position can be strengthened.

Even when we discover that, in a certain matter, we have acted presumptuously, without being commissioned by God, we must not quit—we should repent. There is a difference between quitting and stopping because of repentance. The first is a defeat; the latter is an adjustment that will always result in further victories. Repentance comes because of the truth that sets us free; defeat will result in a spiritual bondage to the power of the enemy.

7. Overcoming Despair

In Genesis 2:18, the Lord said that it was not good for man to be alone. We are social creatures, and when we withdraw from fellowship, we usually sink into the deepest pit of hopelessness—despair. At this point in the downward spiral, we must return to fellowship and get help in reversing the slide or else we will be defeated.

As simple as this may seem, *it is the remedy*. Even though fellow believers can be the source of the enemy's attack on us, we must never run away from the Church. We must rather run to it and work out our problems until they are resolved.

8. Overcoming Defeat

Even if satan's stings of witchcraft have brought such devastation to our lives that we are temporarily defeated, we must see that God can still bring us to ultimate victory. Paul commented to the Corinthians that he had been **"struck down, but not destroyed"** (2 Cor. 4:9). At one point, Paul faced such severe attacks that he **"despaired even of life"** (2 Cor. 1:8), but through it all, he learned that the secret of regaining victory was not trusting in himself, but in **"God who raises the dead"** (2 Cor. 1:9).

Paul wrote, **"...thanks be to God, who gives us the victory through our Lord Jesus Christ"** (1 Cor. 15:57), and, **"in all these things we overwhelmingly conquer through Him who loved us"** (Rom. 8:37). Defeat is not an option in Christ. We will gain victory in that which He has called us to do. The only way we can be defeated is to quit.

Chapter Eleven

COMBATING NEW AGE WITCHCRAFT

The New Age movement is basically a combination of witchcraft and Hinduism, disguised to make it acceptable to white-collar professionals. There is an important reason why this form of spiritualism is targeting this group. For almost 5,800 years of the earth's 6,000 years of recorded history, nearly 95 percent of all workers were agricultural. In just a little over a century, that statistic has been reversed so that now less than 5 percent of the workers in the West are agricultural. This change has been the result of technological advances. The 5 percent who work in agriculture now produce more than the 95 percent could in the last century.

In the mid 1950s, the number of white-collar workers exceeded the number of blue-collar workers in the West. This majority has grown until it is now estimated that blue-collar workers will go the way of agricultural workers, composing only a very small fraction of the population in the near future. When it was predicted that **"…knowledge will increase"** (Dan. 12:4) in the end times, few could have comprehended the degree to which this would happen. Information is now the most valuable commodity in the world, and the job of accumulating, interpreting, packaging, and transferring knowledge has become the world's largest industry.

Those involved in the knowledge industry are not only the most numerous, they are also the wealthiest and most powerful. They are also a group that the Church has become increasingly unsuccessful in reaching, which has made them an appealing target for the New Age movement and other cults. Because people were created to have fellowship with God, who is Spirit, there is a spiritual void in each person that hungers for the supernatural.

The day of supernatural neutrality is over. Those who do not know the true supernatural power of God will become increasingly subject to the evil and counterfeit supernatural powers of the enemy. Those whose doctrines or fears have led them to avoid the supernatural power of God will find themselves, and especially their children, easy prey to evil, supernatural power.

Kingdoms in Conflict

Paul explained, **"For the kingdom of God does not consist in words but in power"** (1 Cor. 4:20). Satan knows this and is therefore quite content to fight the battle on the level of words and doctrines. Regardless of how accurately we can argue doctrinal positions, satan will have little problem conquering us if we do not know the power of God, which is a fundamental aspect of God's Kingdom. Those who truly believe the Bible will walk in power. Righteousness is the result of believing in our hearts, not just in our minds, and those who do not know the power of God only believe in Him in their minds.

Considering the foolish antics of those who have known the power of God in the Pentecostal, Charismatic, Full Gospel, and third wave movements, it is easy to understand why many would shy away from the gifts of the Spirit. But this too is one of the tests that separate the true believers from those who only know creeds or doctrines— God has made the foolish things of the world to confound the wise. Only the humble will be involved in what He is doing, and He will give His grace only to them.

Churches that have rejected the supernatural power of God have become increasingly irrelevant and unable to reach the world, for the battle for people's souls is intensely supernatural in nature. The more secularized society becomes, the more it actually magnifies people's hunger for the supernatural. Consequently, atheists tend to be drawn to the most base forms of witchcraft and the black arts, which they are deceived into thinking are powers resident within people, when actually these powers are demonic in nature.

The denominations and movements within the Church that have rejected the power of God are almost all shrinking because they have become irrelevant and boring, with little or no power to attract converts. Many churches and denominations that have rejected the power of God have already succumbed to influences from the New Age movement. Others are succumbing to the spirit of the age in other forms, not only tolerating the perverted and unbelievers as members, but actually ordaining them as pastors and leaders. Contrary to this, the denominations and movements that preach and walk in the supernatural power of God are not only growing, but are by far the fastest growing religious movements in the world. The apostle Paul declared:

And my message and my preaching were not in persuasive words of wisdom, but in demonstration of the Spirit and of power, so that your faith would not rest on the wisdom of men, but on the power of God (1 Corinthians 2:4-5).

The conflict between the Kingdom of God and the kingdom of evil is not just a conflict between truth and error, but a confrontation of supernatural powers, with both sides seeking to fill the spiritual void in man created by The Fall.

The entire history of God's dealings with humankind has involved demonstrations of supernatural power. It is incongruous to say we are a biblical people and yet not walk in the supernatural power of God. True Christianity is not just a matter of words; it is a demonstration of God's love and power to save, heal, and deliver. Jesus stated that, as the Father had sent Him into the world, so He has sent us into the world (see John 17:18). As our example, Jesus did not just talk about God's power to heal and save; He demonstrated it.

If we are going to preach the Gospel, we must preach it as He did, demonstrating both God's love and power. When Jesus sent out His disciples to preach the Kingdom, they were to heal the sick and cast out demons (see Luke 9:1-2). The Lord never changes; nor does He change the way He sends His true messengers.

Many biblical prophecies concerning the end of the age address the supernatural nature of the conflicts that will occur. A church that does not walk in God's power will become increasingly inadequate to deal with the times and confront the powers that come against it. To overcome the increasing power of the enemy we must **"...desire earnestly spiritual gifts, but especially that you may prophesy"** (1 Cor. 14:1). **"God is spirit, and those who worship Him must worship in spirit and truth"** (John 4:24). Again, the first defense against the deceptive supernatural power of the enemy is to know the true power of God.

Most believers have *some* desire for spiritual gifts, but we must **"earnestly"** desire them if we are going to receive them. Even though most of the Church is now "open" for God to use them in a demonstration of His power, He has decreed that we must *ask, seek,* and *knock* in order to receive (see Matt. 7:7). Those who are just "open" for the Lord to use them are rarely used. Being "open" is usually a cop-out for those who are either too fearful or too prideful to risk failure. It takes faith and persistent seeking if we are to receive.

Pious Delusions

It is often repeated that we are to seek the Giver and not the gifts. That sounds pious, but it is not biblical. Certainly we are to seek the Giver more than the gifts, but we are commanded to seek the gifts too. The two are not mutually exclusive. Seeking to walk in the gifts of the Spirit is actually one form of seeking God, and even more important, it is being obedient. Many such glib statements of apparent wisdom are merely human wisdom and are often in conflict with the Scriptures.

Our God is supernatural, and we cannot truly desire fellowship with Him without desiring fellowship with the supernatural. While many Christians have been hardened by doctrines that justify their powerlessness, claiming that God no longer moves supernaturally, they still long in their hearts for the supernatural. We were all created for fellowship in the Spirit, which is by definition supernatural.

Recently, some of the world's most brilliant theologians and apologists, who believed God no longer works supernaturally, have been won over and are now walking in God's power themselves, often after witnessing just one genuine miracle. *Genuine* is the key word here. Those who sincerely love God and seek to walk in His power are turned off by the fakery and hype often associated with the ministries of those who really do not yet have God's power.

The True Gospel

True Christianity is the true Word of God verified by the true power of God. Jesus went about to **"do and teach"** (Acts 1:1). He usually performed miracles *before* He taught. He knew that people who had an undeniable encounter with God would be far more open to what He said to them. The power Jesus and His apostles demonstrated was used to confirm and illuminate their teachings.

The same is still true. The demonstration of God's power transforms intellectual concepts into a true faith in the teachings of the Lord. It takes both the Word and the power of God to change the inner man. Without both, we may change our outward behavior, but our hearts remain untouched. The spiritual void in the heart must be filled by a true fellowship with God if we are going to be free from the spiritual influence and power of the enemy.

Because witchcraft is counterfeit spiritual authority, we will only be completely free from the power of witchcraft when we are completely submitted to the authority of God. If the spiritual void that is in us is not filled with the real power and authority of God, we will become subject to witchcraft in some form as we draw closer to the end of the age. The Battle of Armageddon is fought in the **"valley of decision"** (Joel 3:14); everyone on earth will be brought to the place of making a decision. It is a power confrontation, and the choice will be made concerning issues of power and authority. We will choose either the power and authority of God or the power and authority of the evil one—but we will all choose.

Discerning Counterfeits

All of the spiritual gifts available to the Church are presently being counterfeited by the enemy. Ironically, those whose lack of faith causes them to avoid spiritual gifts in order to keep from being deceived are *certain* to be deceived. We must walk by faith, not fear, if we are going to stay on the path that leads to life. Fear will inevitably lead us to deception if we allow it to be our motivation.

If we are going to fulfill the purpose of God, it will take a faith like Abraham's, who was willing to risk leaving everything behind in order to seek that which God is building (see Heb. 11:8-10). If we are going to walk in the power of God, we must have more faith in God's ability to lead us into all truth (see John 16:13) than we do in the enemy's ability to deceive us. Faith is the door to fellowship with God. It takes faith to reach beyond the natural realm to the supernatural so that we can see Him who is unseen.

As we walk in faith, what we begin to see with the eyes of our hearts will become more real to us than what we are seeing with our natural eyes. Then we will begin living more for the eternal than for the temporal. Those who walk in true faith are naturally going to appear foolish to those who live according to the wisdom of this world or those who are of a "natural mind."

We take a major step in being delivered from the power of witchcraft when we start to see the Lord so clearly that we respect and serve Him more than anything else. Then we are no longer subject to the influence, manipulation, and control of those who are still earthly-minded or who move in the power of witchcraft.

Those who give themselves to becoming authorities on the nature of evil almost always become darkened and evil in nature themselves. Many "cult watchers" have released a more foul spirit in the Church than the cults they were watching. The paranoia they have promulgated has done more to bring division and damage to the Church than any cult has been able to do. These people have often become the "fault finders" that Jude wrote about, printing and distributing slander and gossip as if it were researched fact. As Jude warned, these are being reserved for the **"black darkness"** (Jude 10-16), in which many of them have already begun to live.

We do not need to study the darkness as much as we need to study the light. Light will always overpower darkness. If we walk in the light, we will cast out the darkness. If we walk in the true supernatural power of God, we will overpower the evil supernatural power as surely as Moses confounded the sorcerers of Egypt. Moses would not have been successful had he gone to Egypt with no power, and neither will we succeed in setting people free today if we are powerless. The increasing power of the enemy will not be effectively confronted and driven out without the power of God.

The Enemy's Strategy

Most cults and New Age groups are now blatantly attacking Christianity, focusing on the Church as the main target of their sorcery. Not only are they infiltrating the Church, but they are using their power to cast spells on those in ministry. In my book, *The Harvest*, I wrote about cult members entering church meetings and performing lewd acts to intimidate and humiliate believers. This has already begun to happen with alarming frequency.

There is a simple solution for churches that have become the target of such attacks—they must seek to know and walk in God's authority and power. He who is in us is much greater than he who is in the world (see 1 John 4:4). As the Church grows in true spiritual authority, the cults are going to fear us far more than we fear them.

Sorcerers usually try to avoid direct confrontation with those who have true spiritual authority. Although they will attack those who are growing in spiritual authority and bearing fruit for the Kingdom of

God, this is generally not done openly, but in secret. The attacks are done indirectly by sacrificing and cursing according to the black arts.

We must recognize the power in satanic sacrifices if we are going to overcome them. In Second Kings 3:27, the king of Moab offered his oldest son as a burnt offering to his demon gods and as a result, **"...there came great wrath against Israel, and they departed..."** (from attacking Moab). It is not biblical for Christians to fear the enemy, but if we do not understand and properly respect his power, we will be vulnerable to his influence.

When combating evil powers, we cannot rely on carnal weapons or mere human strength—neither can we fight on satan's terms. His first strategy in a confrontation is to get us out of the Holy Spirit's control and into a spirit of retaliation. We cannot overcome evil with evil; satan will not cast out satan. Jesus said, **"But if I cast out demons by the Spirit of God, then the kingdom of God has come upon you"** (Matt. 12:28).

This is why Jesus commanded us to **"bless those who curse you..."** (Luke 6:28). Blessings are more powerful than any curse and will quickly overcome them. Even so, it is important for us to recognize when we are being cursed with witchcraft so that we can defend against it and shine light into the darkness that has been directed against us.

Summary

Witchcraft is basically the practice of cursing others. This cursing does not just come through cults or black magic arts; it can come through those who love us and have good intentions but are trying to manipulate us. Using manipulation or a control spirit is a form of witchcraft, regardless of who does it.

The mother who manipulates her son or daughter into marrying her choice has done it through witchcraft, and such relationships usually have to be held together through continued manipulation and control. The prayer group who uses prayers to expose the sins of others is gossiping for the sake of manipulation. This is not genuine prayer—it is witchcraft. Much of what is written in the name of Christian journalism, purportedly as an attempt to keep the Church informed, is gossip and is used to manipulate or gain influence over others. This, too, is witchcraft.

When spiritual leaders use manipulation, hype, or control to build their churches or ministries, they are operating in a counterfeit spiritual authority equivalent to witchcraft. Much of what is taught in business schools is a form of manipulation or control that is witchcraft. Many of the strategies the Church has borrowed from secular journalism and the business world have brought witchcraft into the camp. They must be removed if we are to be free to accomplish our purpose for this hour.

Many of the "yokes" and human expectations that we face have some power of manipulation and witchcraft attached to them. The enemy wants to establish these strongholds to conflict with the calling of God in our lives. However, this is not a license to disregard the expectations of our parents, teachers, or employers. We were known by the Lord before we were born, and many of the influences in our lives have been placed there to help steer us toward our purposes in Him. However, some of the yokes and expectations that well-intentioned parents, teachers, or coaches place upon us must be cast off. When yokes are placed upon us that are not from the Lord, they will become clear as we come to know our calling and purpose in Him because the truth will set us free.

The only yoke that we must take is the Lord's yoke. His yoke is easy and His burden is light (see Matt. 11:28-30). When we take His yoke, we find rest and refreshment instead of the pressure and discouragement that comes from "white" witchcraft. Pressure tactics and manipulation are subtle forms of witchcraft that can have just as much power as the black magic arts. White and black witchcraft may be different branches, but they have the same root and the same deadly poison.

Sadly, even when unstable people recognize the dangers of being subject to charismatic or "white" witchcraft, they will often distort this principle in order to rebel against God's ordained authority over their lives. King Saul is the personification of one who was ordained by God but fell from his place of true spiritual authority to operate in counterfeit spiritual authority. King David, on the other hand, is a personification of true spiritual authority. How did David react to Saul? He was willing to serve in the house of Saul until Saul chased him away. Even then he never retaliated, rebelled, or tried to undermine Saul's authority, but chose instead to honor him as **"the Lord's anointed"** (1 Sam. 24:10).

We need to learn from David's example. Even though he was called to take Saul's place, he never lifted his hand against Saul. David determined that if God had really called him to be the next king then God would have to be the One to establish him. David overcame evil with good by demonstrating the exact opposite of the manipulative or control spirits that had come against him. Had David manipulated his way into the kingdom, he would have almost certainly fallen to witchcraft just like Saul, but David was of a different spirit.

Those who are the target of any form of witchcraft will usually feel the sequence of stings previously listed. If we react to the attack properly, we will not only be free of its influence ourselves, but we can also help to free those who have used witchcraft. The manipulation and control spirits gain entrance through fear. Those who are fearful and insecure are so obsessed with controlling others that they use evil influence, and it will take a demonstration of **"perfect love"** (see 1 John 4:18) to cast out these fears. Jesus commanded us to **"bless those who curse you"** (Matt. 5:44 NKJV). Paul said that we are not to return evil for evil; we are to overcome evil with good (see Rom. 12:19-21).

When we discover that we are the target of witchcraft, retaliation is not the answer. In fact, retaliation is the very thing the enemy would have us do, for it multiplies the evil we are trying to cast out. Satan will not cast out satan; witchcraft will not cast out witchcraft. We must pray for those who are praying against us and bless those who are cursing us. This does not mean we are to bless what they are *doing,* but we must pray that they are delivered from the fears and hatred that motivates them. Pray for your attackers to have a revelation of the perfect love of God. Our greatest victory is in winning those who are in the enemy's grip, not afflicting them in retaliation.

Another source of witchcraft that can be one of the most unexpected causes of our discouragement, confusion, depression, loss of vision, disorientation, and despair is ourselves! When we use manipulation, hype, or control on others, we open ourselves to the consequences. Before we look at others to find the source, we should first look at ourselves. Again, satan cannot cast out satan; we will not be able to cast witchcraft out of others if we are using it ourselves.

Most who have been subject to witchcraft have tried to combat it in the flesh, actually using the same spirit. When we do that, it gains a foothold in our lives that must be broken before we will have the authority to deliver others.

Witchcraft is a serious offense that God will not continue to tolerate in the Church. His intent is to bring down every form and manifestation of witchcraft that ensnares His people. After we have been freed from this terrible evil, we will also be free to walk in the unprecedented power He will entrust to those who walk in true spiritual authority.

Chapter Twelve

WITCHCRAFT IN THE MEDIA

In one of the most remarkable statements made in the New Testament, Peter wrote that we should be **"looking for and hastening the coming of the day of God…"** (2 Pet. 3:12). Obviously, Peter would not have said this if it was not *possible* for us to hasten the coming of the day of God. If we can hasten the coming of His day, it is apparent that we can also *delay* it. Because the enemy knows his time is short, we can be sure that he is doing all he can to keep us from moving in what will hasten the day of the Lord, instead causing its delay.

The harvest will come, and it has already come to many parts of the world. However, there are major stumbling blocks to spiritual advancement that we must address if we are going to receive the full benefit of the impending awakening. These stumbling blocks are not powerful enough to stop revival altogether, but they can limit its scope, depth, duration, and fruit.

The harvest will bring the reaping of everything that has been sown, both good and evil. The harvest that marks the end of this age has already begun, but because many have the concept that the harvest is only a great revival, they do not see it or understand it. The Scriptures teach that the harvest will begin with the tares being taken out first (see Matt. 13:38-40, 49), which has been happening for some time. In many ways, it seems that we have *only* been reaping tares. This has been painful for a season, but the pain will be appreciated when the full harvest begins and we are able to avoid repeating the same mistakes.

One aspect of the harvest of tares that had a significant impact on the international Body of Christ came with the televangelist scandals of recent years. This is not to imply that the individuals involved were "tares." More importantly, the scandals that were brought to light began to uproot some erroneous practices and theologies. Unfortunately, these tares were not exposed by the Church but by the secular news media. As a friend remarked in a roundtable meeting that we hosted, "The Lord is using the secular media to discipline the Church because we have refused to judge ourselves." There is an important truth to this observation.

That the Lord is using the secular media to discipline the Church is a loud warning announcing our fallen condition. Likewise, it is apparent that much of the Church has sincerely given herself to repentance. A sign that this repentance has been genuine enough to be acceptable to God will be when our sovereignty is restored and when the Church is able to judge herself.

Even though the Lord used the heathen nations to discipline Israel for her apostasies, afterward He often destroyed those nations for their arrogance. This may shock our human sensibilities, but those heathen nations were still heathen. They still worshiped idols and would inevitably try to introduce their idol worship to Israel during their occupation.

The same has been happening between the secular media and the Church. Much of the Christian media has been turning to the ways of the secular media. This is not the means by which the Lord intended to discipline the Church, and it will result in even worse consequences if we do not rid ourselves of it.

The Wrong Kind of Repentance

In general, journalism has crossed a line that has made it one of the primary platforms of the **"accuser of our brethren"** (Rev. 12:10). Of course, this would not apply to some journalists, but the foundational principles of modern journalism have married it more to Greek philosophy than to Christianity. Unfortunately, this is also the philosophy that most "Christian" journalists operate by. In fact, the Christian media has at times proven even less honorable and truthful in its reporting than the secular media, causing it to become a major stumbling block to spiritual advancement.

The Christian media is now founded more upon a humanistic philosophy of journalism than upon biblical principles. Through the spirit of *unrighteous judgment*, the Christian media today is one of the greatest sources of deadly poison that is spreading destruction in the Western Church. Although the Lord may have used the media because we would not judge ourselves, the solution is not for us to take on the ways of the heathen, but to return to God's righteous judgment as outlined in His Word.

There is a healthy skepticism that truly *wants* to believe, as the Bereans did when they searched the Scriptures to verify the message of Paul and Barnabas (see Acts 17:11). However, there is another kind of skeptic who only wants to *doubt*. This unhealthy form of skepticism wants to see the worst in others because that somehow makes the skeptic look bigger or at least feel better about his own flaws.

This kind of doubt and cynicism is both tragic and deadly. When the chronicles of this earth are read on that great Judgment Day, we will probably learn that this evil form of doubt was far more deadly than cancer or AIDS. Great souls rise to even greater heights by lifting others higher. Criticism has an appearance of wisdom, but it is wisdom from the dark side, and it is the fruit of the Tree of the Knowledge of Good and Evil.

Since the 1960s, the news media of the West, including the Christian media, seems to have been almost completely taken over by this dark side of skepticism. It is now almost unthinkable for a Christian journalist to write an article about a church, movement, or event without at least throwing in some criticism. This is often done by reporting hearsay or crude gossip as fact, without even contacting the offended parties for their side of the story.

Those who simply pass on gossip are just as guilty of gossiping as those who originated it. All of this is usually done in the name of "the people's right to know," or "to protect people from error." However, are we really protecting them from error by committing one of the most serious errors of all—becoming stumbling blocks?

The Scriptures are shockingly honest about exposing both the good qualities and the flaws in even the greatest spiritual heroes. Yet the Bible was written as history for the sake of instructing others in the ways of God, not for the sake of exposing dirt. How does today's Christian journalism justify its departure from such biblical exhortations as the following?

> **Let no unwholesome word proceed from your mouth, but only such a word as is good for edification according to the need of the moment, so that it will give grace to those who hear** (Ephesians 4:29).

> **If your brother sins, go and show him his fault in private...** (Matthew 18:15).

In Matthew 18, the procedure for addressing sin was given to keep us from becoming stumbling blocks. Not following this procedure, especially in journalism, may have created more stumbling blocks to the Lord's own children than any other source. More damage has probably come to the Church by such journalism, and by so-called "heresy hunting" than has come through the heresies they are trying to expose.

By What Authority?

In his June 8, 1978, commencement address at Harvard University, Alexander Solzhenitsyn said:

> Such as it is, however, the press has become the greatest power within the Western countries, more powerful than the legislature, the executive, and the judiciary. One would then

like to ask: By what law has it been elected and to whom is it responsible?

Solzhenitsyn's question is valid for Western society, but even more so for the Church.

On what basis has the press been granted the extraordinary power it now has? By what authority has it been elected? The Lord appoints elders in the Church to give it both protection and direction. He has set high standards for those elders who would be given such influence. In contrast, we must ask, to whom are the Christian journalists accountable, and to what standards must they be held? These are important questions.

Just as the secular media can now manipulate public opinion and dictate policy, sometimes even more effectively than our elected officials, Christian journalists can do the same in the Church. Who gave them this power? Is it derived merely from an ability to be articulate or because of the anointing and commission of God? Do we have the right to exert a massive influence in the Church simply because we have the marketing ability to distribute our magazines, newsletters, or programs?

James warned, **"Let not many of you become teachers, my brethren, knowing that as such we will incur a stricter judgment"** (James 3:1). It is a most serious matter to have influence in the Lord's own household. Let us be very careful how we attain it and use it.

Paul explained that he did not presume to go beyond the sphere of authority that was appointed to him (see 2 Cor. 10:14-18). He realized that God has given each of us certain realms of authority and grace, and we need to take care that we don't go beyond these appointed realms.

Where Are the Elders?

Much of what is done today by Christian journalism and the heresy hunters encroaches upon the realm of authority that was given to the elders of the Church. The very meaning of the word *elder* implies a certain degree of longevity in faithful service to the Church before one is given this influence. The position of elder is the highest and most respected office appointed in the biblical Church.

Journalists today, on the other hand, are often not accountable to anyone. Even though they are not required to comply with any of the biblical standards for leadership in the Church, they can have more influence through the media than even the most anointed true elders.

Writing can be an aspect of a biblical ministry, and there are journalists who have obvious spiritual ministries as teachers, pastors, and so forth. Some of these have been faithful to the biblical standards required for leaders in the Church, and they should be recognized as elders in the Body of Christ. For such people, journalism can be a proper platform for the authority they have been given by God. Even so, they too can become stumbling blocks if they do not comply with the biblical procedures for bringing correction in the Church.

Most of those who are sources of the prevailing critical spirit or spirit of unrighteous judgment are not standing on true anointing, but on a platform of influence gained by other means. Some received their position because of professional training, which came from schools founded upon a humanistic philosophy of journalism. This philosophy does have the appearance of wisdom and the search for truth, but it is actually in conflict with the Truth Himself. Others may have been given a true commission from God but have compromised with the spirit of the world.

John said, **"...the whole world lies in the power of the evil one"** (1 John 5:19). The ways of the world are not the ways of God, as Paul exhorted the Ephesians.

...In reference to your former manner of life, you lay aside the old self, which is being corrupted in accordance with the lusts of deceit, and that you be renewed in the spirit of your mind, and put on the new self, which in the likeness of God has been created in righteousness and holiness of the truth (Ephesians 4:22-24).

If we are going to be **"created in righteousness and holiness of the truth,"** we must put on a new self and live by a different philosophy than that of the world.

Good Intentions

Many Christian journalists entered the field with the intention of trying to provide an alternative source of information to the secular media. This is a noble vision and is truly needed. The Church is called to be the pillar and support of the truth. However, the accuracy level of reporting in Christian journalism has not proven to be any higher than in secular journalism—it only has a more "spiritual" slant to it.

The investigative reporting done by Christian journalists on the events that I have personally witnessed, or about the people I know, has been shockingly dishonest and untrue. Some were so prone to the use of gossip, hearsay, or even apparent imagination that they could rival some of the grocery counter tabloids. Truth is our most precious commodity, and we cannot continue to allow it to be compromised, or we will receive the judgment that is promised for such deception.

In an article printed in a Christian magazine about myself and our ministry, we struggled to find a single fact that was accurate. Even the positive things they had to say were distorted to the degree that we had a hard time understanding what they were talking about. When we tried to find out how it had gotten so far off track, it became obvious that their research was as flawed as the tabloids. Anything labeled Christian should have integrity that greatly exceeds the world's standards rather than falling to their lowest level.

I went to the owner of this magazine, and he listened patiently, but never once acknowledged a mistake. I never sensed any malice on his or the writer's part. A drunken driver may not have any malice in his heart toward the people that he kills, but they are just as dead. Carelessness kills, and drunken driving kills more people than murderers do each year. The media is intoxicated right now with its own power and influence, and they are hurting many people with their drunken carelessness.

Those who have been influenced by the humanistic philosophy of journalism may think we are shallow, blind, or duped if we do not expose the wrongs of others when we write about them. Yet it is much better to be ridiculed by people than it is for God to think of us as stumbling blocks. We all must stand in front of the judgment seat of Christ, and those who are trying to sit in it now, without authority, will have a most difficult time on that day.

The world's methods for seeking truth are very different from the way that real truth is found. Truth is only found in Jesus, and it can only be found when we are being led by the Holy Spirit. Secular schools may be able to teach us something about the mechanics of writing or the technical knowledge needed to understand today's media tools, but the philosophy that is sown into their students is devastating when incorporated into Christian media.

Judgment on Journalism

Christian television ministries have come under severe judgment in the last few years. Television has given vastly more influence to some people in the Church than God ever intended them to have. Whenever we move beyond the sphere of authority that has been appointed to us by God, we have moved beyond grace, and we are bound to fall.

Other forms of Christian media are about to experience the same scrutiny that the television ministries have undergone. The Lord will ultimately deal with the secular media as well, but **"...it is time for judgment to begin with the household of God..."** (1 Pet. 4:17). Christian journalism will soon come under the same kind of judgment that television ministries have been experiencing.

For a period of time, the public's trust and esteem of televangelists probably sank lower than that of any other professional group, including politicians and lawyers. There are, of course, politicians and lawyers who live their lives by the highest standards of integrity, and they, too, must bear the judgment of their profession because there are fundamental roots in these professions that must be corrected. Likewise, many journalists who sincerely attempt to live by the highest standards of truth and integrity are often trying to do so on a foundation that simply will not support the truth. That is why the very foundations are being shaken—so that only that which cannot be shaken will remain (see Heb. 12:25-28).

We will soon enter a period when Christian magazines, journals, newsletters, and newspapers and the like will all come under the most intense pressure and scrutiny. The exposers are about to be exposed, and they will receive back the same measure of judgment that they measured out to others. Even those who have tried to be honest and fair, but have been operating on a humanistic foundation, will see their faulty foundations collapse.

Can this judgment be avoided? The Scriptures clearly teach that judgment can be avoided by genuine repentance. Paul told the Corinthians, **"But if we judged ourselves rightly, we would not be judged"** (1 Cor. 11:31). Repentance is more than requesting forgiveness for our wrongs—repentance is going back to where we missed the turn and getting back on the right road. It also often includes restitution for the wrongs that have caused injury to others.

We must remember that the harvest is the reaping of what has been sown, and, **"For in the way you judge, you will be judged; and by your standard of measure, it will be measured to you"** (Matt. 7:2). If we have sown unrighteous judgments, then judgment will soon come upon us. If we want to reap grace, however, we should use every opportunity that we can to sow grace. If we desire to reap mercy, we must use every opportunity to sow mercy. **"Do not be deceived, God is not mocked; for whatever a man sows, this he will also reap"** (Gal. 6:7).

The Grace of True Authority

According to the many examples in the New Testament, there are times when the errors of certain movements or sects must be addressed. The Lord Himself warned His disciples saying, **"…beware of the leaven of the Pharisees…"** (Matt. 16:6). Major portions of the Book of Galatians and other apostolic letters are devoted to correcting mistakes in doctrine or practice. The main difference between these scriptural examples and what is so often done today is that the biblical writers had the *authority* to bring the needed correction.

One reason there is so much wrong judgment, or needed correction that is given in the wrong spirit or manner, is the vacuum that exists because those who truly have been given authority by God have refrained from using it. This does not justify the wrong use of authority or the presumption of those who try to bring correction to the Church without having the authority, but it does make such actions more understandable. We can even appreciate the courage that some have shown by addressing issues that no one else would address, but that still does not make it right. Even worse, it puts those courageous people in jeopardy of becoming stumbling blocks. Paul's lament to the Corinthians still applies to the Church today:

> **Or do you not know that the saints will judge the world? If the world is judged by you, are you not competent to constitute the smallest law courts? Do you not know that we shall judge angels? How much more matters of this life** (1 Corinthians 6:2-3).

Possibly the main reason the Church is so full of unrighteous judgment is because there is no format for *righteous* judgment in the Church. Until the elders take their proper places in the gates, churches will continue to be subject to the judgment of the secular media and heresy hunters. Regardless of how well-intentioned these groups may be, they sow division and unrighteous judgment, which wounds the Body of Christ, more than they rectify the errors they seek to expose.

The Lord has given mandates to the Church that we cannot accomplish without unity. Righteous judgment is one of them. This issue must be addressed by Church leaders on every level if we are going to accomplish our mandate for this hour. Unrighteous judgment is a source of most of the conflicts in the world. Since the Church is called to be the light of this world, we should have the answers to the world's problems. But how can we help to bring righteous judgment to the world if we cannot even judge ourselves?

Because of the many excesses of the past or the tendency of some to presume authority beyond their appointed jurisdiction, it is easy to understand why we tend to shy away from this difficult issue. However, until we cease our continued neglect of this basic mandate—to provide righteous judgment to the Church and then through the Church to ourselves—we will continue to be subject to the unrighteous judgment of the world.

Part III

THE
RELIGIOUS SPIRIT

Chapter Thirteen

UNDERSTANDING THE RELIGIOUS SPIRIT

L oving God is the greatest commandment and the greatest gift that
we can receive. The second greatest commandment is to love our
neighbors. As the Lord affirmed, the whole law is fulfilled by keeping these two commandments, which means that, if we keep these two
commandments, we will keep the whole law (see Matt. 22:34-40;
Rom. 13:8). If we love the Lord, we will not worship idols. If we love
our neighbors, we will not envy them, steal from them, murder them,
and so forth. Therefore, keeping these two positive commandments to
love will enable us to obey all of the negative "do nots" of the law.

Simple love for God will overcome most of the evil in our hearts,
and it is the most powerful weapon against evil in the world. Because
loving God is our highest goal, it must be the primary focus of our
lives. To divert us from this ultimate quest, the enemy uses one of his
most deceptive and deadly attacks upon the Church through the religious spirit. The devil wants to keep us focused on the evil in our
lives, knowing that we will become what we are beholding (see 2 Cor.
3:18). As long as we keep looking at the evil, it will continue to have
dominion over us. On the contrary, when we look to the Lord and
behold His glory, we will be changed into His image.

This is not to imply that we should ignore the sins and errors that
are in our lives. In fact, the Scriptures command us to examine ourselves and test ourselves to be sure that we are still in the faith (see
2 Cor. 13:5). The issue is what we do after the iniquity is discovered.
Do we turn to the Tree of the Knowledge of Good and Evil or to the
Tree of Life? Do we try to make ourselves better so that we will then

be acceptable to God, or do we turn to the cross of Jesus to find both forgiveness and power to overcome the sin?

A primary strategy of the enemy is intended to keep us focused on the evil, partaking of the Tree of Knowledge, and to keep us away from the glory of the Lord and the cross. This tactic comes in the form of a religious spirit, an evil spirit that is the counterfeit of the true love of God and true worship. This guise for true religion has probably done far more damage to the Church than the New Age movement and all other cults combined.

The Nature of a Religious Spirit

A religious spirit is a demon that seeks to substitute religious activity for the power of the Holy Spirit in our lives. Its primary objective is to have the Church **"holding to a form of godliness, although they have denied its power…"** (2 Tim. 3:5). The apostle Paul completed his exhortation with **"avoid such men as these."** This religious spirit is the **"…leaven of the Pharisees and Sadducees"** (Matt. 16:6) of which the Lord warned His disciples to beware.

The Lord often used metaphors to illustrate the lessons He taught. The religious spirit operates like the leaven in bread, which does not add substance or nutritional value to the bread—it only inflates it. Such is the byproduct of the religious spirit. It does not add to the life or power of the Church, it merely feeds the very pride of man which caused the first fall and almost every fall since.

Satan seems to understand even better than the Church that **"…God resists the proud, but gives grace to the humble…"** (James 4:6 NKJV). He knows very well that God will not inhabit any work that is inflated with pride and that God Himself will even resist such a work. Satan's strategy is to make us proud—even proud of good things, such as how much we read our Bibles, witness, or feed the poor. He knows that, if we do the will of God in pride, our work will be counterproductive and could even ultimately work toward our fall.

Satan also knows that, once leaven gets into the bread, it is extremely difficult to remove. Pride, by its very nature, is the most difficult stronghold to remove or correct. A religious spirit keeps us from hearing the voice of God by encouraging us to assume that we already know God's opinion, what He is saying, and what pleases Him. This delusion is the result of believing that God is just like us. A religious spirit encourages the rationalization of Scripture, having us believe that rebukes, exhortations, and words of correction are for other people but not for us.

If a religious spirit is a problem in your life, you have probably already begun to think about how badly someone you know needs to read this chapter. It may not even have occurred to you that God put this book into your hands because you need it. In fact, we all need it. This is one enemy that all of us are battling to some degree. It is imperative that we get free of this devastating deception and stay free. We will not be able to worship the Lord in Spirit and truth until we do.

The degree to which we have been delivered from this powerful deception will directly affect the degree to which we are able to preach the true Gospel in power. The Church's confrontation with the religious spirit will be one of the epic battles of the last days. Everyone will be fighting in this battle. The only issue to be determined is which side we will be on.

We will never have the authority to deliver others from darkness until we are free from it ourselves. To begin taking ground from this vast enemy, we must ask the Lord to shine His light on us, showing how this applies to us personally. As illustrated by the Lord's continual confrontations with the Pharisees, the Church's most desperate fight from the very beginning has been with this spirit. Just as the primary characteristic of the Pharisees was focusing on what was wrong with others while being blind to their own faults, the religious spirit tries to make us do the same.

The Great Deception

One of the most deceptive characteristics about the religious spirit is that it is founded upon zeal for God. We tend to think that zeal for God could only be good, but we need to consider *why* we are zealous for Him.

Paul wrote of his Jewish brethren in Romans 10:2: **"For I testify about them that they have a *zeal* for God, but not in accordance with knowledge."** No one on earth prayed more, fasted more, read the Bible more, had a greater hope in the coming of the Messiah, or had more zeal for the things of God than the Pharisees. Yet, they were the greatest opposers of God and His Messiah when He came.

The young Saul of Tarsus was motivated by zeal for God while he was persecuting His Church. Zeal for God is one of the most desperately needed characteristics of the Church today, most of which is bound by a terrible Laodicean lukewarmness. The Lord commanded the Laodicean church to **"...therefore be zealous and repent"** (Rev. 3:19).

Those who are truly zealous are the most difficult to stop, so the enemy's strategy against them is to push them too far. His first step is to persuade them to glory in their own zeal. Regardless of how important our characteristics or gifts may be, if the enemy can get us to take pride in them, he will have caught us in his snare, and they will be used for evil.

The Lord had little trouble with demons while He walked the earth. They quickly recognized His authority and begged for mercy. It was the conservative, zealous, religious community that immediately became His greatest enemy. Those who were the most zealous for the Word of God crucified the Word Himself when He became flesh to walk among them. The same is still true.

All of the cults and false religions combined have not done as much damage to the moves of God as the opposition, or infiltration, of the religious spirit in the Church. Cults and false religions are easily discerned, but the religious spirit has thwarted or diverted possibly every revival or movement to date, and it still retains a seat of honor throughout most of the visible Church.

It is a manifestation of the religious spirit that will take its seat in the very temple of God, declaring itself to be God (see 2 Thess. 2:4). The temple of God is no longer made with hands, and this is not speaking about a building in Jerusalem. This man of sin will take his seat in the Church. Tragically, it will be the Church that allows him to do so.

The Two Foundations

Like most of the enemy's strongholds, the religious spirit builds its work on two basic foundations: fear and pride. *The religious spirit seeks to have us serve the Lord in order to gain His approval, rather than receiving approval through the cross of Jesus.* Therefore, those with a religious spirit will base their relationship with God on personal discipline or performance, rather than on the propitiatory sacrifice of Christ. The motivation for doing this can be fear or pride or a combination of both.

Fear and pride are the two basic results of The Fall, and our deliverance from them is usually a long process, which is why the Lord even gave Jezebel **"time to repent"** (Rev. 2:20-21). The biblical Jezebel, the wife of King Ahab, was a very religious woman, but she was given to false religion. The Lord gave Jezebel in the Book of Revelation time to repent because the roots of this spirit go so deep that time is required to fully repent and be delivered from it.

However, even though the Lord gave Jezebel time to repent, He rebuked the church of Thyatira for *tolerating* her (see Rev. 2:20). We can be patient with people who have religious spirits, but we must not tolerate their ministry in our midst while we are waiting. If this spirit is not confronted quickly, it could do more damage to the Church, our ministries, our families, and our lives, than any other assault that we may suffer.

The Foundation of Guilt

Eli, the priest who raised the prophet Samuel, is a biblical example of someone who ministered in a religious spirit founded upon guilt. Eli had so much zeal for the Lord that when he heard that the Ark had been captured by the Philistines, he fell over and died. He had spent his life trying to serve the Lord as a high priest, but the very first prophetic word given to Samuel was one of the most frightening rebukes given in the Scriptures—and it was directed to Eli:

> **For I have told him that I am about to judge his house forever for the iniquity which he knew, because his sons brought a curse on themselves and he did not rebuke them. Therefore I have sworn to the house of Eli that the iniquity of Eli's house shall not be atoned for by sacrifice or offering forever** (1 Samuel 3:13-14).

Eli's zeal for the Lord was based on sacrifices and offerings intended to compensate for his irresponsibility as a father. Guilt can spur us on to great zeal for the Lord, and our sacrifices and offerings can become an attempt to atone for our failures. This is an affront to the cross, which alone can atone for our guilt. Such zeal will never be acceptable to the Lord, even if we could make sacrifices forever.

We should note here that the Lord never said that Eli's sin couldn't be forgiven. He said that Eli's attempts to atone for sin *by sacrifice and offering* would never succeed. There are multitudes of men and women whose zeal for the Lord is likewise based on an attempt to atone for sin, failure, or irresponsibility in other areas of their lives. But all the sacrifices in the world will not atone for even our smallest failure. To even make such an attempt is an insult to the cross of Jesus, which is the only acceptable sacrifice to the Father for sin.

Attempting to gain God's approval by our own sacrifice opens the door wide for a religious spirit because such service is not based on the blood of Jesus, but on an attempt to make our own atonement for sin. This does not mean we should not do things to please the Lord; it means our motive for pleasing the Lord is for His joy, not for our acceptance. One is God-centered; the other is self-centered. This is self-centeredness of the most destructive kind—an attempt to circumvent the cross.

It is also noteworthy that one of the sins of Eli's sons was that they **"...despised the offering of the Lord"** (1 Sam. 2:17). They appropriated for their own selfish use the sacrifices and offerings brought to the Lord. Those who are gripped by this form of a religious spirit will often be the most zealous to preach the cross, but herein lies the perversion. They emphasize *their* cross more than the cross of Jesus. Their real delight is more in self-abasement than in the cross of Christ, which alone makes us righteous and acceptable to God.

The Foundation of Pride

Idealism is one of the most deceptive and destructive disguises of the religious spirit. Idealism is of human origin and is a form of humanism. Although it has the appearance of seeking only the highest standards and the preservation of God's glory, idealism is possibly the most deadly enemy of true revelation and true grace. It is deadly because it does not allow for growing up into grace and wisdom; rather it attacks and destroys the foundation of those who are in pursuit of God's glory but are not yet there.

Idealism imposes on others standards that are beyond what God has required or given the grace for at that time. For example, people controlled by this kind of religious spirit may condemn those who are not praying two hours a day as they are. The truth is, it may be God's will for us to be praying that much, but how we get there is crucial. The grace of God may first call us to pray just ten minutes a day. Then, as we become so blessed by His presence, we will not want to quit after ten minutes but instead spend more and more time with Him until we pray for an hour, then two. When we are eventually praying two hours a day, it will be because of our love for prayer and the presence of the Lord, not out of fear or pride.

A person with a religious spirit based on idealism will usually seek the perfect church and will refuse to be a part of anything less. Those led by the Holy Spirit may also have high hopes for a church but will still be able to give themselves in service to even some of the most lowly works in order to help those works grow in vision and maturity. The Holy Spirit is called **"the Helper"** (John 14:26), and those who are truly led by the Spirit will always be looking for ways to help, not to stand aloof and criticize.

When a religious spirit is founded upon pride, it is evidenced by *perfectionism*. The perfectionist sees everything as black or white. This develops into extremes, requiring that every person and every teaching be judged as either 100 percent right or 100 percent wrong. This is a standard that only Jesus could comply with. It will lead to a serious delusion when we impose it on ourselves or others. True grace imparts a truth that sets people free, showing them the way out of their sin and beckoning them to higher levels of spiritual maturity.

One with a religious spirit can usually point to problems with great accuracy, but seldom has solutions, except to tear down what has already been built. This is the strategy of the enemy to nullify progress that is being made and to sow discouragement that will limit future progress. This produces the mentality that, if we cannot go straight to the top of the mountain, we should not climb at all, but just "die to self." This is a death that God has not required, and it is a perversion of the exhortation for us to take up our crosses daily.

The perfectionist both imposes and tries to live by standards that stifle true maturity and growth. The grace of God will lead us up the mountain step-by-step. The Lord does not condemn us because we may trip a few times while trying to climb. He graciously picks us up with the encouragement that we can make it. We must have a vision of making it to the top and should never condemn ourselves for not being there yet, *as long as we are still climbing.*

James said, **"…we all stumble in many ways…"** (James 3:2). If we had to wait until we were perfect before we could minister, no one would ever qualify for the ministry. Even though perfect obedience and understanding should always be our goals, such will never be found within ourselves, but only as we come to perfectly abide in the Perfect One.

Because **"now we see through a glass, darkly"** (1 Cor. 13:12 KJV), or in part, we must always be open to greater accuracy in our beliefs and teachings. One of the greatest delusions of all is that we are already complete in our understanding or 100 percent accurate in our perceptions or actions. Those with a religious spirit will usually claim to be open to more understanding, but most of the time this is done to convince *everyone else* to be open to what they teach, while they remain steadfastly closed to others.

Jesus blessed Peter and turned the keys of the Kingdom over to him just before He had to rebuke him by calling him "satan" (see Matt. 16:23). Right after this greatest of blessings, the enemy deceived him, yet the Lord did not take the keys away from Peter. In fact, Jesus knew when He gave the keys to Peter that he would soon deny even knowing Him.

Many years after Peter used the keys to open the door of faith for both the Jews and Gentiles, "the least of the apostles," Paul, had to rebuke him publicly because of his hypocrisy (see 1 Cor. 15:9; Gal. 2:11-14). Even so, Peter was promised that he would sit on one of the 12 thrones judging the 12 tribes of Israel (see Matt. 19:28). The Lord has proven that He will commission and use people long before most of us would, and when He calls us, He already knows all the mistakes that we will make.

It seems that the Lord's leadership style was to provide a place where His followers could make mistakes and learn from them. If we require our children to be perfectly mature while they are still children, it stifles their growth and maturity. The same is true in the Church. We must correct mistakes, because that is how we learn, but it must be a correction that encourages and frees, not one that condemns and crushes initiative.

The Deadly Combination

One of the most powerful and deceptive forms of the religious spirit is built upon the foundations of both fear and pride. Those who are bound in this way go through periods of deep anguish and remorse at their failures, but this false repentance results only in more self-abasement and further attempts to make sacrifices that will appease the Lord. Those bound by this religious spirit often flip to the other side where they become so convinced that they are superior to other Christians or other groups that they become unteachable and unable to receive reproof. The foundation that they stand on at any given time will be dictated more by external pressure than by true conviction.

Such a religious spirit is so slippery that it will wiggle out of almost any attempt to confront it. If you address the pride, the fears and insecurities will rise up to attract sympathy. If you confront the fear, it will then change into religious pride masquerading as faith. This type of spirit will drive individuals or congregations to such extremes that they will inevitably disintegrate.

The Counterfeit Gift of Discernment

A religious spirit will usually give a counterfeit gift of discernment of spirits that is motivated by suspicion and fear. This counterfeit gift thrives on seeing what is wrong with others, rather than seeing what God is doing so we can help them along. Using this type of discernment, a religious spirit can cause some of its greatest damage to the Church. Its ministry will almost always leave more damage and division than healing, reconciliation, and building. Its wisdom is rooted in the Tree of the Knowledge of Good and Evil, and though the truth may be accurate, it is ministered in a spirit that kills.

Suspicion is rooted in such things as rejection, territorial preservation, or general insecurity. The true gift of discernment can only function through love. Any motive other than love will distort spiritual perception. Whenever someone submits a judgment or criticism about another person or group, we should disregard it unless we know that the one bringing it truly loves that person or group and has an "investment" of service to them.

Summary

As you have probably already deduced, all evil spiritual strongholds have similar characteristics. Their tactics and functions often overlap to become a web that captures and then holds its prey. Of all the fortresses of deception that the enemy has built among people, the religious spirit has been the most deceptive and deadly because it comes as a pretense of righteousness and goodness.

Even though this spirit comes with a pretense for righteousness, it always has us looking at ourselves, trying to measure ourselves against standards, comparing ourselves to others, and consequently distracting us from the glory of God that transforms us. The religious spirit is therefore the most concentrated fruit from the Tree of the Knowledge of Good and Evil. The "good" side of this tree is just as deadly as the evil—the fruit of the religious spirit will always be spiritual death. In the next chapters, we will study other manifestations of this spirit, how it gains entry into our lives, and how we can be free from it.

Chapter Fourteen

ANGELS OF LIGHT

When Paul warned the Corinthians about those who ministered in a religious spirit, which sought to bring a yoke of legalism upon the young Church, he explained that:

> **For such men are false apostles, deceitful workers, disguising themselves as apostles of Christ. No wonder, for even Satan disguises himself as an angel of light. Therefore it is not surprising if his servants also disguise themselves as servants of righteousness...** (2 Corinthians 11:13-15).

In this text, Paul was specifically writing about those from among the Jews who were seeking to bring the Gentile converts under the yoke of the Law of Moses. This was the first and most deadly heresy to impose itself on the young Church. It has been compared to the temptation of Eve, since the Church is called to be the Bride of Christ, the "last Adam." So this was a second attempt by the devil to seduce the Bride to partake of the Tree of Knowledge again. It succeeded with many during that time. Paul and the other apostles wrote large portions of the New Testament to combat this deception, warning believers that the result of turning back to the Law of Moses would actually sever them from Christ (see Gal. 5:4). It is noteworthy that this same heresy is arising again among some Messianic groups.

The phraseology often used by the apostles in the first century was that there were "false apostles" or "angels of light." Satan's most deceptive and deadly disguise is to come as a servant of righteousness, using truths for the purpose of destruction. The devil is quite skillful at quoting Scripture and using wisdom, but it is the wisdom of the Tree of Knowledge—wisdom that kills.

Because Paul was the champion of grace and the pure message of the Gospel, the modern form of this heresy most especially undermines his New Testament letters, while at the same time persuading different people groups that they are the descendants of ten "lost tribes of Israel." This false doctrine urges people to base their identity on the flesh instead of on the Spirit, as those born again into Christ. This sounds ridiculous to those who are well-grounded in the New Covenant, but tragically, many Christians are not well-grounded. This heresy effectively severs many from a true relationship to Jesus through the cross. If it has not yet attacked your church, it almost certainly will.

This new form of the original heresy to seduce the Church into turning to the Law of Moses for righteousness is but one form in which these "angels of light" come. All who are empowered by a religious spirit will have a tendency to get us focused on what is wrong with Christians or the Church, rather than on what is right. Although this spirit usually comes in the guise of protecting the sheep, the truth, or the Lord's glory, it is an evil, critical spirit that will always end up causing division and destruction.

Criticism has an appearance of wisdom, but it is pride in one of its most base forms. When we criticize someone, we are in effect declaring ourselves to be better than them. We may be better than others in some areas, but if we are, it is only by grace. Believers who recognize the true grace of God never look for ways to put others down, but rather find ways to build them up. As an old proverb declares, "Any jackass can kick a barn down, but it requires a skillful carpenter to build one."

The Religious Spirit and Murder

When Adam and Eve chose to live by the Knowledge of Good and Evil, they were partaking of the religious spirit. The first result of this was self-centeredness—they started looking at themselves. The first child born to them after they partook of this fruit was Cain, who is the first biblical model of a man controlled by the religious spirit.

"...Cain was a tiller of the ground" (Gen. 4:2) or earthly-minded. The religious spirit will always seek to keep us focused on the earthly realm, rather than the heavenly realm. The "seed of Cain" judges by what is seen and cannot understand those who **"...endured, as seeing Him who is unseen"** (Heb. 11:27).

In Revelation 13:11, we see the second beast **"coming up *out of the earth.*"** This is because the spiritual seed of Cain emphasizes tilling the ground. This earthly-mindedness has produced one of the most evil beasts the world will ever know.

Cain also tried to make an offering to the Lord from his own labors. God rejected that sacrifice but accepted Abel's sacrifice of blood. The fruit of our labors will never be an acceptable offering to the Lord. This was a statement from the beginning that God would only accept the blood of the Lamb. Instead of receiving this correction and repenting, Cain became jealous of his brother and killed him (see Gen. 4:1-15). Those who attempt to live by their own works will often become enraged at those who take their stand on the righteousness of the Lamb.

That is precisely why Saul of Tarsus, the Pharisee of Pharisees, was so enraged against Christians. They represented the greatest threat to that on which the Pharisees had built their whole lives. Because of this, the Pharisees could not endure the very existence of the Christians. Religions that are based on works will easily become violent. This includes "Christian" sects where a doctrine of works has supplanted the cross of Christ.

The Lord said that, if a man hates his brother, he is guilty of murder (see Matt. 5:21-22). Those who are driven by religious spirits may well try to destroy people by means other than the physical taking of their lives. Many of the onslaughts of slander instigated against churches and ministries are the ragings of this same religious spirit that caused Cain to slay his brother.

The Test of a True Messenger

In Ezekiel 37, the prophet was taken to a valley full of dry bones and asked if the bones could live. The Lord then commanded him to **"prophesy over these bones"** (Ezek. 37:4). As he prophesied, they came together, came to life, and then became a great army.

This is an important test that every true ministry must pass. The true prophet can see a great army in even the driest of bones. He will prophesy life to those bones until they come to life and then become an army. A false prophet with a religious spirit will do little more than just tell the bones how dry they are, heaping discouragement and condemnation on them, while imparting no life or power to overcome their circumstances.

Apostles and prophets are given authority to build up and tear down, but we have no right to tear down if we have not first built up. We should give no one the authority to bring correction to the people under our care unless they first have a history of providing spiritual nourishment and building people up. Some may say that such a policy would eliminate the ministry of the prophets altogether, but I say that so-called "prophets" who do not have a heart to build people up *should be* eliminated from ministry. Jude said they are grumblers, fault finders who are **"hidden reefs in your love feasts"** (see Jude 12-16).

Even so, as we can see from Eli's tragic example, God promises woe to the shepherds who feed and care for the sheep but fail to *correct* them. The true grace of God is found between the extremes of unrighteous faultfinding and unsanctified mercy (approving of things that God condemns). Either extreme can be the result of a religious spirit.

Chapter Fifteen

OTHER MASKS
OF THE RELIGIOUS SPIRIT

What is popularly called the "Jezebel spirit" is a form of the religious spirit. Just as Jezebel was the ambitious and manipulative wife of King Ahab—a weak leader who allowed her to dictate policy in his kingdom—the Jezebel spirit will usually be found supplanting weak leadership. The Jezebel spirit usually gains its dominion by making political alliances and often uses a deceptively humble and submissive demeanor in order to manipulate. However, once this spirit gains authority, it will usually manifest a strong control spirit and shameless presumption. Despite its name, this spiritual problem is not limited to women.

Jezebel **"calls herself a prophetess"** (Rev. 2:20). Often one of the telltale signs of false prophets who are operating in a religious spirit is that they are preoccupied with their own recognition. To the degree that self-seeking and the need for recognition abides within us, our ministry will be corrupted. Those who are easily offended because they are not given an important title or position should never be accepted by that title or given that position. The key difference between those motivated by a desire for recognition and those motivated by love for the Lord is the difference between the false prophet and the true. As we read in John 7:17-18, those who seek their own recognition speak from themselves, but those who are seeking the recognition of the One who sent them are true.

Demanding recognition for herself, Jezebel serves as the enemy of the true prophetic ministry. Jezebel was the greatest enemy of one of the Old Covenant's most powerful prophets, Elijah, whose ministry especially typified preparing the way for the Lord. The Jezebel spirit is one of the most potent forms of the religious spirit, which seeks to keep the Church and the world from being prepared for the return of the Lord.

The Jezebel spirit especially attacks the prophetic ministry because that ministry has an important place in preparing the way for the Lord. This is why John the Baptist was persecuted by a personification of Jezebel in the wife of Herod (see Mark 6:14-29). The prophetic ministry is the primary vehicle through which the Lord gives timely, strategic direction to His people. Jezebel knows that removing the true prophets will make the people vulnerable to her false prophets, which always results in idolatry and spiritual adultery.

When there is a void of hearing the true voice of the Lord, the people will be much more susceptible to the deceptions of the enemy. This is why Jesus called the religious leaders of His own day **"blind guides"** (Matt. 23:16 NKJV). These men, who knew the Messianic prophecies better than anyone else in the world, looked into the face of the One who perfectly fulfilled those prophecies and thought that He was sent from Beelzebub.

Jezebel's prophets of Baal were also given to sacrifice, even to the point of cutting and flailing themselves while seeking the manifestation of their god. A primary strategy of the religious spirit is to get the Church devoted to "sacrifice" in a way that perverts the command for us to take up our crosses daily. This perversion will have us putting more faith in our sacrifices than in the Lord's sacrifice. It will also use sacrifices and offerings to pressure God to manifest Himself. This is a form of the terrible delusion that we can somehow purchase the grace and presence of God with our good works.

The Root of Self-righteousness

We do not crucify ourselves for the sake of righteousness, purification, spiritual maturity, or to get the Lord to manifest Himself; this is nothing more than conjuring. We are **"crucified with Christ"** (Gal. 2:20). If we "crucify ourselves," the only result is self-righteousness—which is pride in one of its most base forms. This pride is deceptive because it gives the appearance of wisdom and righteousness, of which the apostle Paul warned:

> **Let no one keep defrauding you of your prize by delighting in self-abasement and the worship of the angels, taking his stand on visions he has seen, inflated without cause by his fleshly mind, and not holding fast to the head, from whom the entire body, being supplied and held together by the joints and ligaments, grows with a growth which is from God. If you have died with Christ to the elementary principles of the world, why, as if you were living in the world, do you submit yourself to decrees, such as, "Do not handle, do not taste, do not touch!" (which all refer to things destined to perish with use)—in accordance with the commandments and teachings of men? These are matters which have, to be sure, the appearance of wisdom in self-made religion and self-abasement and severe treatment of the body, but are of no value against fleshly indulgence** (Colossians 2:18-23).

The religious spirit will make us feel good about our spiritual condition as long as it is self-centered and self-seeking. Pride feels good; it can even be exhilarating. But it keeps our attention on how well we are doing and on how we stand compared to others—not on the glory of God. Consequently, we put our confidence in discipline and personal sacrifice rather than in the Lord and His sacrifice.

Of course, discipline and a commitment to self-sacrifice are essential qualities for every believer to have. Even so, it is the motivation behind them that determines whether we are being driven by a religious spirit or by the Holy Spirit. A religious spirit motivates through fear and guilt or through pride and ambition. The motivation of the Holy Spirit is love for the Son of God.

Delighting in self-abasement is a sure symptom of the religious spirit. This does not mean we can neglect to discipline ourselves, fast, or buffet our bodies as Paul did (see 1 Cor. 9:27). However, the problem comes when we take a perverse delight in this rather than delighting in the Son of God.

Deceptive Revelation

Colossians 2:18-19 indicates that a person with a religious spirit will tend to delight in self-abasement and will often be given to worshiping angels or taking improper stands on visions he has seen. A religious spirit wants us to worship anything or anyone but Jesus. The same spirit that is given to worshiping angels will also be prone to excessively exalting people.

We must beware of anyone who unduly exalts angels, men and women of God, or anyone who uses the visions he has received in order to gain improper influence in the Church. God does not give us revelations so that people will respect us more or to prove our ministries. The fruit of true revelation will be humility, not pride.

Of course, the Scriptures teach that Christians do have prophetic experiences, and we are told in Acts 2:17 that they will increase in the last days. Jesus also warned that in the last days there would be many false prophets (see Matt. 24:11). Prophetic revelation that is truly from God is crucial to the Body of Christ. The enemy knows this very well, which is why he will raise up many false prophets. But they can be easily discerned. As Paul warned the Colossians, the danger does not come from those who are *having* prophetic revelations, but from those who have been *inflated* by them.

A religious spirit will always feed our fear or pride; whereas, genuine spiritual maturity will always lead to increasing humility. This progression of humility is wonderfully demonstrated in the life of the apostle Paul. In his letter to the Galatians, estimated to have been written in A.D. 56, he declared that when he visited the original apostles in Jerusalem, they **"…contributed nothing to me"** (Gal. 2:6). By this he was declaring that he had as much as they did.

In Paul's first letter to the Corinthians, written about six years later, he called himself the **"least of the apostles"** (1 Cor. 15:9). In Ephesians 3:8, written in about A.D. 61, he declared himself to be **"the very least of all saints."** When writing to Timothy in approximately A.D. 65, Paul declared himself to be the foremost of all sinners (see 1 Tim. 1:15), adding that he had found mercy. A true revelation of God's mercy is a great antidote for the religious spirit.

It is clear by these Scriptures that the great apostle was not completely free of pride in the first years of his ministry. Which of us can claim to be free of it either? However, we are all hopefully growing in grace and, therefore, humility.

Young apostles may exude a lot of pride, but they can still be true apostles. The key here is in which direction we are heading. Are we being puffed up by our revelations, our commissions, or our accomplishments? Or are we growing in grace and humility?

The Martyr Syndrome

When combined with the religious spirit, the martyr syndrome is one of the ultimate and most deadly delusions. To be a true martyr for the faith and literally lose our lives for the sake of Christ is one of the greatest honors that we can receive in this life. Yet when this is perverted, it is a most tragic form of deception.

When a religious spirit is combined with the martyr syndrome, it is almost impossible for that person to be delivered from the deception that he is "suffering for the Gospel." At this point, any rejection or correction received from others is perceived as the price he must pay to "stand for the truth." This warped perspective will drive him even further from the truth and any possibility of correction.

The martyr syndrome can also be a manifestation of the spirit of suicide. It is sometimes easier to "die for the Lord" than it is to live for Him. Those who have a perverted understanding of the cross glory more in death than they do in life. They fail to see that the point of the cross is the resurrection not the grave.

Self-help Psychology

There is a "self-help psychology" movement that is attempting to replace the power of the cross in the Church. Humanistically-based psychology is what Paul calls **"a different gospel"** (see 2 Cor. 11:4); it is an enemy of the cross and is another form of the religious spirit. Paul also warned:

> **Therefore as you have received Christ Jesus the Lord, so walk in Him, having been firmly rooted and now being built up in Him and established in your faith, just as you were instructed, and overflowing with gratitude. See to it that no one takes you captive through philosophy and empty deception, according to the tradition of men, according to the elementary principles of the world, rather than according to Christ** (Colossians 2:6-8).

We all need "inner healing" to some degree, but much of what is being called inner healing is nothing more than digging up the "old man" and trying to get him healed. The answer to these deep wounds is not a procedure or a formula but simple forgiveness. When we go to the cross and find forgiveness and true acceptance based on the blood of Jesus, we will find a perfect love able to cast out all our fears and wash away all bitterness and resentment.

This seems too simple, and that is why Paul said: **"…I am afraid that, as the serpent deceived Eve by his craftiness, your minds will be led astray from the simplicity and purity of devotion to Christ"** (2 Cor. 11:3). Salvation is simple. Deliverance is simple. Yet one of the enemy's major strategies is diluting the power of the Gospel by having us add to it, which is how Eve was deceived. We add to it because we do not think it is acceptable unless it somehow seems brilliant or abstract. This is precisely why we must become like children to enter the Kingdom (see Matt. 18:3).

The Lord commanded the man and woman not to eat from the Tree of the Knowledge of Good and Evil because they would die. When the serpent asked about this command, Eve replied that they could not eat from the tree **"or touch it"** (Gen. 3:3). However, the Lord had not said anything about refraining from touching the tree.

Adding to God's commandments is just as destructive as taking away from them. Anyone who thinks that he can so flippantly add to the Word of God does not respect it enough to keep it when the testing comes. If satan can get us to either add or subtract from the Word, then he knows our fall is imminent, just as it was for Eve.

Although there are many "Christian" philosophies and therapies that seem wise, most are in fact attempting to be substitutes for the Holy Spirit in our lives. Some people do need counseling, and there are outstanding Christian counselors who do lead people to the cross. But others are simply leading people into a black hole of self-centeredness that will consume them and try to suck in everyone else around them as well. In spite of the Christian terminology, this philosophy is an enemy of the cross of Christ.

Chapter Sixteen

THE WARNING SIGNS
OF A RELIGIOUS SPIRIT

The following is a list of some of the most obvious warning signs of the religious spirit. As stated, almost everyone is battling the religious spirit at least to some degree, and everyone's fight is somewhat different. One may be dealing with all the issues listed below to a small degree and yet be more free from the yoke of the religious spirit than one who has serious problems with just a couple of them.

Our goal is to be completely free of any influence from the religious spirit by being fully submitted to the Holy Spirit. Without complete submission to the Lord, there is no way to be free from the religious spirit.

People with a religious spirit:

1. *Will often see their primary mission as the tearing down of whatever they believe is wrong.* Such a person's ministry will result more in division and destruction than in lasting works that bear fruit for the Kingdom.

2. *Will be unable to accept a rebuke, especially from those they judge to be less spiritual than themselves.* Think back on how you responded to the last few times someone tried to correct you.

3. *Will have a philosophy that, "I will not listen to people but only to God."* Since God frequently speaks through people, this is an obvious delusion, revealing serious spiritual pride.

4. *Will be inclined to see more of what is wrong than what is right with other people, other churches, etc.* From the valley, John saw

Babylon, but when he was carried to a high mountain, he saw the New Jerusalem (see Rev. 21:10). If we are seeing only Babylon, it is because of our perspective. Those who are in a place of true vision will have their attention on what God is doing, not people.

5. *Will be subject to an overwhelming feeling of guilt that they can never measure up to the Lord's standards.* Guilt is a root of the religious spirit because it causes us to base our relationship with Him on our performance rather than on the cross. Jesus has already measured up for us. He is the completed work that the Father is seeking to accomplish within us. Our whole goal in life should be simply to abide in Him.

6. *Will keep score on their spiritual life.* This includes feeling better about ourselves because we go to more meetings, read our Bibles more, do more things for the Lord, etc. These are all noble endeavors, but the true measure of spiritual maturity is getting closer to the Lord.

7. *Will believe that they have been appointed to fix everyone else.* These persons become the self-appointed watchmen or sheriffs in God's Kingdom. They are seldom involved in building, but serve only to keep the Church in a state of annoyance and agitation, if not causing serious divisions.

8. *Will have a leadership style that is bossy, overbearing, and intolerant of the weakness or failure of others.* James said:

> **But the wisdom from above is first pure, then peaceable, gentle, reasonable, full of mercy and good fruits, unwavering, without hypocrisy. And the seed whose fruit is righteousness is sown in peace by those who make peace** (James 3:17-18).

9. *Will have a sense that they are closer to God than other people or that their lives or ministries are more pleasing to Him.* This is a symptom of the profound delusion that we draw closer to God because of who we are rather than through Jesus.

10. *Will take pride in their spiritual maturity and discipline, especially as compared to others.* True spiritual maturity involves growing up into Christ. When we begin to compare ourselves to others, it is obvious that we have lost sight of the true goal—Jesus.

11. *Will believe that they are on the "cutting edge" of what God is doing.* This includes thinking that we are involved in the most important thing that God is doing.

12. *Will have a mechanical prayer life.* When we start feeling relief that our prayer time is over or that we have finally prayed through our prayer list, we should consider our condition. We will never feel relief when our conversations are over with the One we love.

13. *Will do things in order to be noticed by people.* This is a symptom of the idolatry of fearing people more than we fear God, which results in a religion that serves people instead of God.

14. *Will be overly repulsed by emotionalism.* When people who are subject to a religious spirit encounter the true life of God, it will usually appear to them to be excessive, emotional, and carnal. True passion for God is often emotional and demonstrative, such as David exemplified when he brought the ark of God into Jerusalem (see 2 Sam. 6:14-16).

15. *Will use emotionalism as a substitute for the work of the Holy Spirit.* This seems contradictory to the previous point, but the religious spirit will often take contradictory positions in its drive for self-preservation and exaltation. This use of emotionalism will include such things as requiring weeping and wailing as evidence of repentance, or "falling under the power" as evidence that one has been touched by God. Both of these can be evidences of the true work of the Holy Spirit, but when we require these manifestations, we are beginning to move in another spirit.

At Jonathan Edwards' meetings during the First Great Awakening, some of the toughest, most rebellious men would fall to the ground and stay there for up to 24 hours. They got up changed, however, and such strange manifestations of the Holy Spirit fueled the Great Awakenings. Even so, Edwards stated that people faking the manifestations did more to bring an end to the Great Awakening than did the enemies of the revival!

16. *Will be encouraged when their ministries look better than others.* We could also include in this being discouraged when it seems that others are looking better or growing faster than they are.

17. *Will glory more in what God did in the past than in what He is doing in the present.* God has not changed—He is the same yesterday, today, and forever. The veil has been removed, and we can be as close to God today as anyone ever has been in the past. A religious spirit will always seek to focus our attention on works and on making comparisons, rather than on simply drawing closer to the Lord.

18. *Will tend to be suspicious of or opposed to new movements, churches, etc.* This is an obvious symptom of jealousy, a primary fruit of the religious spirit or the pride that asserts that God would not do anything new without doing it through us. Of course, those with such a mentality are seldom used by the Lord to birth new works.

19. *Will tend to reject spiritual manifestations that they do not understand.* This is a symptom of the pride and arrogance of presuming our opinions are the same as God's. True humility keeps us teachable and open, patiently waiting for fruit before making judgments. True discernment enables us to look for and hope for the best, not the worst. For this reason, we are exhorted to **"...examine everything carefully; hold fast to that which is good,"** (1 Thess. 5:21) not what is bad.

20. *Will overreact to carnality in the Church.* The truth is, there is probably far more carnality in the Church and a lot less of the Holy Spirit than even the most critical person has guessed. It is important that we learn to discern between them in order to be delivered from our carnality and to grow in our submission to the Holy Spirit. The critical person will annihilate those who may still be 60 percent carnal but who were 95 percent carnal last year. Instead, we need to recognize that

people are making progress and do what we can to help them along the way.

21. *Will overreact to immaturity in the Church.* There is an immaturity that is acceptable to the Lord. A 2-year-old is immature when compared to a 9-year-old, but that is to be expected; and in fact, he may be very mature for a 2-year-old. The idealistic religious spirit only sees the immaturity, without considering the other important factors.

22. *Will be overly prone to view supernatural manifestations as evidence of God's approval.* This is just another form of keeping score and comparing ourselves with others. Some of Jesus' greatest miracles, such as walking on water, were seen by only a few. His works were done to glorify the Father not Himself. Those who use the evidence of miracles to promote and build their own ministries and reputations have made a serious departure from the path of life.

23. *Will be unable to join anything that they do not deem perfect or nearly perfect.* The Lord joined and even gave His life for the fallen human race. Such is the nature of those who abide in Him.

24. *Will be overly paranoid of the religious spirit.* We do not get free of something by fearing it but by overcoming it with faith in Christ Jesus.

25. *Will have the tendency to glory in anything but the cross of Jesus, what He has accomplished, and who He is.* If we are building our lives, ministries, or churches on anything else, we are building on a shaky foundation that will not stand.

Check Yourself

While reading through this list, if you thought continually of how it relates to someone else, but really could not see how much it applies to you, you may have the biggest problem of all. Those with a religious spirit usually have such a "log in their own eye" that they cannot see their own problems (see Matt. 7:3). Again, as Paul exhorted us: **"Test yourselves to see if you are in the faith..."** (2 Cor. 13:5).

First, He did not say to "test your neighbor" or to "test your pastor," but to **"test yourselves."** Using this test to measure others can be a symptom that we have a serious problem.

If this list has given you illumination about problems in another person, church, or ministry, be sure that you respond in the Holy Spirit, heeding Paul's warning to the Galatians:

> **Brethren, even if anyone is caught in any trespass, you who are spiritual, restore such a one in a spirit of gentleness; each one looking to yourself, so that you too will not be tempted** (Galatians 6:1).

It is the tendency of a religious spirit to separate us from other believers. Therefore, the tendency to cut off fellowship with anyone because they have these problems is an indication that we have a problem ourselves. Love helps. The Holy Spirit is called "the Helper" because that is His nature (see John 14:16). If we are following the Holy Spirit, helping will always be our tendency when someone else has problems.

Chapter Seventeen

Ten Things We Can Do to Get Free of the Religious Spirit

I have been somewhat reticent to try to formulate this list for obvious reasons: those who are bound by a religious spirit may tend to interpret this list in a manner that promotes more religious activity in place of true intimacy with the Lord. However, I trust that if you have the humility to read this, the Lord will give you His grace to use this list properly—as suggested guidelines to help us draw closer to Him.

1. *Develop a secret relationship with the Lord.* The Lord warned His disciples not to be like the Pharisees who did their works to be noticed by people but to do their works in secret before the Father. In this way, we begin to put our hope and trust in our relationship to Him not people. There is no greater security than to know that we are known by God. As the Lord warned, **"How can you believe, when you receive glory one from another and you do not seek the glory that is from the one and only God"** (John 5:44). Seeking glory or recognition from people is probably the most destructive thing that we can do to true faith.

2. *Pray that the same love with which the Father loved the Son would be in you.* The Lord Jesus Himself prayed for the same love with which the Father loved Him to be in us (see John 17:26). We know that this prayer of the Son of God, who was in perfect harmony with the Father, will be answered. But we have not because we ask not (see James 4:2). When this love replaces religious duty, our good works will greatly exceed what they would be without it.

3. **"Study to shew thyself approved unto God** [not people]" (2 Tim. 2:15 KJV). When we study the Word of God in order to demonstrate our knowledge before people or to prove our position before others, we have departed from the Spirit of Truth that leads to truth. The Spirit of Truth came to reveal Jesus not us. We must study His Word in order to seek Him and to do what is approved by Him, not others. As the Lord warned the Pharisees, **"...You are those who justify yourselves in the sight of men, but God knows your hearts; for that which is highly esteemed among men is detestable in the sight of God"** (Luke 16:15). If we are motivated to do the things that are highly esteemed by people or to justify ourselves before others, we will be doing that which is detestable in God's sight.

4. *Spend quality time alone with the Lord each day. Endeavor, as much as it is possible, to increase this time to the place where you spend more time alone with the Lord than with any other individual.* When we are spending time with Him continually, we will not be so prone to the guilt that drives us to start measuring our spiritual lives by our works.

5. *Seek to hear the voice of the Lord every day.* The Lord's sheep know His voice (see John 10:27). They know His voice because they spend time with Him. If a good earthly parent seeks to spend some quality time with their children each day, how much more does the Lord seek to spend quality time with us? The quality of the time can be measured by the quality of the communication. The Lord really does want to speak to all of us each day. If we would refuse to go to bed until we have heard from Him in some meaningful way, our lives would quickly change. The most important thing that we can do each day is to spend time with Him and hear from Him. Do not just seek to hear the words of the Lord but the Word Himself.

6. *Ask the Lord to give you the love for your neighbors that He has for them.* Only then will our witness and our ministry to them be pure. But we must always endeavor to love the Lord first and foremost. If we love the Lord more than we do our children, or our neighbors, we will love them more than we would otherwise.

7. *Seek to turn your criticisms into intercession.* Your first response to seeing something wrong with someone else should be to pray for them, asking for grace on their behalf. If some people especially irritate you, endeavor to pray for them even more. If you make an investment in them in prayer—**"For where your treasure is, there your heart will be also"** (Matt. 6:21)—you will start to genuinely love them. True spiritual authority is founded on love; so if you love them enough, the Lord may be able to trust you with the ministry of truth that will set them free. Some of the greatest spiritual victories that are counted in Heaven are the ones that turn enemies into friends and turn those who dwell in darkness into children of the light. This must always be our goal.

8. *Continually ask the Lord to see His glory.* It is by seeing His glory with an unveiled face that we are changed into His same image (see 2 Cor. 3:18). Understanding doctrine is important, but until we see His glory, it remains only doctrine. When we behold Him, the doctrine will become our nature. It is not by believing in our minds but in our hearts that results in righteousness.

9. *Keep as one of your highest goals to manifest the sweet aroma of the knowledge of God in every place* (see 2 Cor. 2:14). Like Moses, ask the Lord not to send you anywhere that His manifest presence is not going to go with you (see Exod. 33:15). We should only want to be where He is, and we should always behave as is befitting in the presence of the King.

10. *When you have failed to do any of the things listed above properly, ask forgiveness,* **"...forgetting those things which are behind...press toward the mark for the prize of the high calling of God in Christ Jesus"** (Phil. 3:13-14 KJV).

Conclusion

Basically, the religious spirit seeks to replace the Holy Spirit as the source of spiritual life. It does this by seeking to replace true repentance, which leads to grace, with a repentance based on our performance. The effect is to replace true humility with pride.

True religion is based on loving the Lord and then loving our neighbors. True religion will promote discipline and obedience founded on love for the Lord rather than the need or desire for recognition or acceptance. The wife who keeps herself in shape because she loves her husband will be easily distinguished from the one who does it because of her own ego. The former will carry her beauty with grace and dignity; the latter may be physically appealing, but it will be a seductive appeal that is a perversion of true love.

The religious spirit is basically a manifestation of the "good" side of the Tree of the Knowledge of Good and Evil. When Adam and Eve ate of that tree in the Garden, the first result was that they looked at themselves. Self-centeredness is the poison which made that fruit deadly, and it is still the most deadly poison the serpent seeks to give us. In contrast with the religious spirit, which causes us to focus our attention on ourselves and base our concept of the Christian life on performance, the Holy Spirit will always lead us into a life that is Christ-centered.

The Holy Spirit produces fruit by joining us to the Lord and applying the work He accomplished for us on the cross: **"For the word of the cross is foolishness to those who are perishing, but to us who are being saved it is the power of God"** (1 Cor. 1:18). However, we must understand that this is the cross of Christ—not our own cross. We are called to deny ourselves and take up our crosses daily, but we are not to glory in self-abasement or to try to live by the virtue of our own sacrifices. Rather, we are to glory in what Jesus accomplished and the sacrifice that *He* made (see Phil. 3:3).

We have our standing before God solely on the basis of the cross of Christ. Our ability to come boldly before the throne of God has nothing to do with whether we have had a good or bad day or how properly we have performed all of our religious duties. Our acceptance before God and our ability to come into His presence is based on one thing only—the sacrifice that Jesus made for our justification.

His sacrifice does not negate the need for personal holiness, for as James asserted, **"...faith, if it has no works, is dead..."** (James 2:17). If we are joined to Christ, we will not go on living in sin. However, we do not become free from sin in order to abide in Him but by abiding in Him. Jesus is the Way, the Truth, and the Life. If He is not our Life, then we do not really know the Way or the Truth either. It is the religious spirit that tries to keep Christianity in the realm of the Way and the Truth, while keeping us from the essential union by which Jesus becomes our Life. True Christianity involves not just *what* we believe, but *who* we believe.

True worship does not have as its purpose to see the Lord—rather, worship comes from having seen Him. When we see Him, we will worship. When we see His glory, we will no longer be captivated by our own positive or negative qualities—our souls will be captured by His beauty. When the Lamb enters, even the 24 elders will cast their crowns at His feet (see Rev. 4:10). That is the goal of true faith—to see Him, to abide in Him, and to reveal Him.

The world is becoming increasingly repulsed by religion. However, when Jesus is lifted up, all people will be drawn to Him (see John 12:32). Because the whole creation was created through Him and for Him, we all have a Jesus-sized hole in our soul. Nothing else will ever satisfy the longing of the human heart or bring us peace—except a genuine relationship with Christ Jesus.

When we are truly joined to Jesus, unstoppable living waters begin to flow out of our innermost beings (see John 7:38). As more and more people are freed and this water begins to flow in them, it will become a great river of life in the midst of the earth. Those who drink from this river will never thirst again; they will have found satisfaction for the deepest yearning of the human soul. The more we get free of the religious spirit, the purer and clearer these waters will be.

WHERE DO WE GO FROM HERE?

This book is a basic study of three strongholds. After reading this book, hopefully you were able to think of many other applications and manifestations of these evil powers. My goal was to lay a foundation of general knowledge upon which the Holy Spirit could build an even greater understanding. These "revelations" are arrows in your quiver. Use them wisely.

For information about the ministry of Rick Joyner and other books and materials that are available from him, visit the website at www.morningstarministries.org or call 1-800-542-0278 for a free catalog.

STUDY GUIDE

CONTENTS

How to Use This Study Guide

P-R-A-Y
Prepare

1. Get into a framework of spiritual warfare by finding a quiet place to focus your heart with thanksgiving, praise, and worship.
2. Using the title of the chapter you are reading, ask the Lord to give you a humble heart to see what you need to see and hear. Confess anything that comes to mind as you pray.
3. Ask the Holy Spirit to be your Teacher and to help you consider your life in light of His Word as you go through your study time.

Read

1. Read the chapter, highlighting important parts that have particular meaning to your life.
2. Make notes of anything you need to apply to your life in the margins.
3. Also, jot down any areas that the Holy Spirit earmarks as needing prayer.

Apply

1. Look over anything you highlighted and reread these sections.
2. Using the notes you made in the margins, make any areas of application into goals by creating a list and a target date of completion.

Goal: (We have suggested some goals for the first six chapters to get you started.)

Goal:

Goal:

3. Answer the questions provided as a means of reviewing the material and creating the repetition necessary to have greater retention and understanding of these principles.

Yield

1. Take the goals you have listed in the Apply section and pray over them. Ask the Holy Spirit to strengthen you to the task ahead as you grow in His likeness through these goals.
2. Devote prayer time to any areas that the Holy Spirit earmarked as needing prayer. Look up Scriptures that speak to these areas and pray them over your life. Ask someone close to you to pray with you in any area that seems overwhelming to you.

Remember, the goal of the book is for you to become more intimate with God, not to set up a formula or religious duty that replaces God or amplifies the religious spirit's activity in your life. Use the guide to direct you toward personal interaction with the Lord.

Introduction

Satan's Cord of Three Strands

P-R-A-Y
Prepare

1. Get into a framework of spiritual warfare by finding a quiet place to focus your heart with thanksgiving, praise, and worship.
2. Using the title "Satan's Cord of Three Strands," ask the Lord to give you a humble heart to see what you need to see and hear. Confess anything that comes to mind as you pray.
3. Ask the Holy Spirit to be your Teacher and to help you consider your life in light of His Word as you go through your study time.

Read

1. Read the Introduction, highlighting important parts that have particular meaning to your life.
2. Make notes of anything you need to apply to your life in the margins.
3. Also, jot down any areas that the Holy Spirit earmarks as needing prayer.

Apply

1. Look over anything you highlighted and reread these sections.
2. Using the notes that you made in the margins, make any areas of application into goals by creating a list and a target date of completion.

Goal: Here is a sample: Have no fear of evil. Premise: If I am walking in the light, I will fear no evil, but all evil will be in fear of me. I will do the following to conquer the fears I have:

    a. I will look up at least ten Scriptures about fear and write them on small cards for my use. (11/20)

b. I will pray each one of the Scriptures each day for 30 days. (12/20)

c. I will take time at the end to evaluate the Word's effect on my fear. (12/21)

Goal:

Goal:

3. Answer the questions provided as a means of reviewing the material and creating the repetition necessary to have greater retention and understanding of these principles.

Answer the following:

1. "These three (racism, witchcraft, and the religious spirit), working together in a deadly alliance, can be seen at the root of almost all the death and destruction that has been the bane of human history." Consider major events in history in America and around the world (i.e., the Holocaust, the Civil War in America, etc.). Do you see these three prevalent in the events you name? Explain. _____

_____

_____

2. Why do you think the threefold cord of racism, witchcraft, and the religious spirit is "very difficult to break when they work together?"

_____

_____

3. When we study to understand the ultimate evil forces, what should we also endeavor to understand? Why? _____

4. In your experience, how does truth set us free? How does truth break the power of evil? What are the results in the life of the believer? _____

_____

_____

Fill in the blanks:

5. When an unclean spirit goes out of a person, it will try to _____ if the place it left is not _____. Not only will it ____ , but it will also bring _____ other _____ _____ more _____ than itself.

6. Our goal must be to not just cast out the _____, but to _____ the place it occupied with the ____ of the ____ _____.

7. The best way to drive out evil and _____ is with ____—the ____ to deception.

8. We reveal what is wrong and reveal God's _____ and _____ that will drive out the _____.

9. Our goal is not only to pass the ____, but to bear ____ ____. We do this by first getting ____ ourselves and then setting others ____ of these evil _____.

10. We must understand how racism, witchcraft, and the religious spirit work _____. Because of these ____ and cross _____, we need to study all three ____.

Matching:

11. a. We are not warring against _____   1) grace to the humble.
    b. We are warring against _____   2) Humility.
    c. God gives _____   3) flesh and blood.
    d. We must walk in _____   4) servants of those who are not yet free.

    e. We are to be the _____   5) evil forces that control people.

True or False:

12. Spiritual warfare is not for everyone.
13. Truth is fundamental to all true followers of Christ.
14. It is the calling of all Christians to rule and reign with Christ.
15. When we reach Heaven, we will begin our training for rulership.
16. We have been given powerful weapons to destroy the works of the devil.
17. Determine the one statement that is incorrect below:
    a.   The battle we are engaged in is a good fight.

b. We have been entrusted with divinely powerful weapons that no evil can stand against.

c. The battle is for our sake, so that we can grow in character and faith.

d. One Christian who walks in truth can be the most powerful force on earth.

e. We must spend more time trying to ward off attacks of the enemy.

18. Read First Peter 5:6-10. Write it below, adding your name at appropriate places, such as where there are pronouns.

<u>Humble yourself, John, therefore, under the mighty hand of God, that He may exalt you, John, at the proper time....</u>

Yield

1. Take the goals you have listed in the Apply section and pray over them. Ask the Holy Spirit to strengthen you to the task ahead as you grow in His likeness through these goals.

2. Devote prayer time to any areas that the Holy Spirit earmarked as needing prayer. Look up Scriptures that speak to these areas and pray them over your life. Ask someone close to you to pray with you in any area that seems overwhelming to you.

Part I

RACISM

Chapter One

THE ULTIMATE POWERS OF EVIL

P-R-A-Y

Prepare

1. Get into a framework of spiritual warfare by finding a quiet place to focus your heart with thanksgiving, praise, and worship.
2. Using the title "The Ultimate Powers of Evil," ask the Lord to give you a humble heart to see what you need to see and hear. Confess anything that comes to mind as you pray.
3. Ask the Holy Spirit to be your Teacher and to help you consider your life in light of His Word as you go through your study time.

Read

1. Read Chapter One, highlighting important parts that have particular meaning to your life.
2. Make notes of anything you need to apply to your life in the margins.
3. Also, jot down any areas that the Holy Spirit earmarks as needing prayer.

Apply

1. Look over anything you highlighted and reread these sections.
2. Using the notes you made in the margins, make any areas of application into goals by creating a list and a target date of completion.

Goal: Here is a sample: I will overcome my bias against those who do not speak English clearly. Premise: If I walk in humility, I will not be able to feel anything but love for all people.

a. I will spend an hour in prayer, asking God to reveal the roots of my bias. (3/16)

b. For the next 30 days, I will speak an extra word of kindness to everyone who has a foreign accent. (4/10)

c. I will visit a church prayer meeting of another culture and learn the people's names so I can pray for them. (4/1)

Goal:

Goal:

3. Answer the questions provided as a means of reviewing the material and creating the repetition necessary to have greater retention and understanding of these principles.

Answer the following:

1. Explain the roots of the stronghold of racism. Where is it rooted? What are the two ultimate yokes that hold people in bondage? How does deception play into this stronghold within the Church and spiritual movements that emerge? _____

_____

_____

2. What two powers have controlled humankind since The Fall? How do these powers elicit racism? _____

3. How are fear and pride a part of the end of the age, as Jesus spoke in Matthew 24:7? Explain this Scripture in light of ethnic differences. _____

_____

4. Why is it impossible to stop racism through legislation or human agency? What role does the Church have in overcoming racism in the world?_____

_____

5. If the Church does not overcome racism and take authority, what will be the result? Explain Luke 21:25-26 in light of this. _____

_____

_____

6. What is your sense of the status of racism in worldclass cities today? In cultures and nations? _____

True or False:

7. Psalm 65:5,7 describes how the Lord demonstrated His power to calm the storm and the sea.
8. The Lord will again calm the roaring sea with His Word.
9. We have been sent to watch the Lord destroy the works of the devil.
10. Racism is one of the ultimate enemies of the truth, the Gospel, and humankind.
11. The Church will not be able to conquer racism.
12. Racism is a principality.
13. Racism empowers the spirit of death.
14. When Jew and Gentile are grafted together in Christ, it will mean the overcoming of death.

Fill in the blanks:

15. There are ____ foundations of racism: 1) ____ in the flesh – judging others by _____ and feeling _____ within ourselves, and 2) _____ due to the separation between God and man as a result of the ____, we are ____, afraid of those who are ____ and those we cannot ____.
16. Fear breaks _____ just as ____ is the bridge that _____ relationships. You can have love and even genuine _____, but if you do not have ____, a relationship is not ____. Trust is torn down by ___ and ____, creating _____.
17. The ____ of Christ confronts and ____ both the pride of ____ and his _____. The revelation of our sin drives us to the ____ to find _____ and _____. This destroys our ___ and establishes our ____ on the Savior, which also restores our ____ in Him.
18. The deeper the cross ___ in us, the more ____ we become and the more ____ in His love. It works a ____ in us for those who are _____ than our nature. We begin to judge from a ____ perspective, not after the ____.
19. Second Corinthians 5:16-17: **"Therefore from now on we recognize no man according to the _____; even though we have**

known ____ according to the flesh, yet now we know Him thus
___ ____. Therefore if any man is in ____, he is a ___ ____; the
old things ____ ___; behold, ____ things have come."
20. Isaiah 11:2-3: "The Spirit of the Lord will ____ on Him, the
spirit of ____ and ____, the spirit of ____ and ____, the spirit of
____ and the ___ of the Lord. And He will ____ in the ___ of the
Lord, and He will not ____ by what His ____ ____, nor make
a ____ by what His ___ ____."

Multiple Choice (there may be more than one correct answer):

21. One of the primary reasons we miss the Lord when He tries to draw
near to us is because:
    a. we are caught up in spiritual waves
    b. we tend to know the Lord after a form rather than by the Spirit
    c. we only recognize Him if He approaches us in a form that we
are used to
    d. we can only see Him clearly in Heaven
22. According to Matthew 23:39, we will not see the Lord until we
learn to:
    a. make a pact with others to pray daily
    b. trust in our godly instincts
    c. make huge gains in the area of brotherly love
    d. bless those whom He sends to us, regardless of the form in
which they come
23. According to Mark 11:17, the Church is to be:
    a. a house of prayer for all nations
    b. the ultimate antithesis to racism, totally integrated
    c. a place where people will be unified again
24. Speaking in tongues is the antithesis to the tower of Babel because:
    a. tongues are a sign to end racism after the scattering of Babel
    b. tongues help the Church understand the meaning of the Spirit
    c. tongues provoke questions among unbelievers
    d. tongues show that every convert, from any cultural background
or sex, has an equal standing before God
25. When the Church truly worships Jesus:
    a. people will need to have the worship explained because it will
be different from their culture

   b. people will be drawn to Him

   c. people will understand everything about the Scriptures

   d. people will understand with one heart

26. Eliminate the one statement below that is incorrect:
   a. There are differences in our standing before God in governmental authority.
   b. Newly born-again Christians can go as boldly before God's throne as the greatest preacher.
   c. God does not show partiality.
   d. There are differences in our standing before God in terms of race, sex, and cultural background.

27. Choose which one of the statements below is true:
   a. The gates of hell have nothing to do with access points in our lives.
   b. Racism is one of the biggest doors the evil one now has into the world.
   c. Those who escape racism are incapable of shutting the gates of hell.
   d. Being free of racism replaces humility and faith with fear and pride.

Yield

1. Take the goals you have listed in the Apply section and pray over them. Ask the Holy Spirit to strengthen you to the task ahead as you grow in His likeness through these goals.

2. Devote prayer time to any areas the Holy Spirit earmarked as needing prayer. Look up Scriptures that speak to these areas and pray them over your life. Ask someone close to you to pray with you in any area that seems overwhelming to you.

Chapter Two

THE TYRANNY OF THE FAMILIAR

P-R-A-Y
Prepare

1. Get into a framework of spiritual warfare by finding a quiet place to focus your heart with thanksgiving, praise, and worship.
2. Using the title "The Tyranny of the Familiar," ask the Lord to give you a humble heart to see what you need to see and hear. Confess anything that comes to mind as you pray.
3. Ask the Holy Spirit to be your Teacher and to help you consider your life in light of His Word as you go through your study time.

Read

1. Read Chapter Two, highlighting important parts that have particular meaning to your life.
2. Make notes of anything you need to apply to your life in the margins.
3. Also, jot down any areas that the Holy Spirit earmarks as needing prayer.

Apply

1. Look over anything you highlighted and reread these sections.
2. Using the notes you made in the margins, make any areas of application into goals by creating a list and a target date of completion.

Goal: Here is a sample: I will overcome my judgmental spirit toward the opposite sex. Premise: If I claim to have Christ in me, I must walk in the revelation of how He treated others. My hurts and disappointments with the other sex will limit my ability to grow in Christlikeness if I do not rid myself of the stereotypical thoughts.

    a. I will study one Bible character of the opposite gender each day for seven days to see how God used them for His glory. (6/4)

    b. I will identify and pray for those of the opposite sex who irritate me the most for 30 days, asking God to show me my weakness and asking the Lord's blessing upon them. (6/15)

    c. I will plan at least one act of kindness toward a member of the opposite sex during the next 30 days. (6/15)

Goal:

Goal:

3. Answer the questions provided as a means of reviewing the material and creating the repetition necessary to have greater retention and understanding of these principles.

Answer the following:

1. How does the tyranny of the familiar affect ethnic groups?_____

_____

2. Why do we so easily come into the bondage of the familiar? _____

_____

3. What must take place to institute true change in our lives? _____

_____

4. Why are most people unwilling to build the trust necessary to get out of their situation?_____

Matching:

5. a. Israel preferred the flesh pots _____   1) not emptying from vessel to vessel.

    b. Moab was undisturbed _____   2) bring impurities to the surface.

    c. Commotion and stirring _____   3) over the supernatural provision of God.

d. When we are thrust into change _____   4) we will be
                                              more pure.

e. When we settle down after a change _____   5) many things
                                              begin to surface.

Multiple Choice (there may be more than one correct answer):

6. Crime and violence can usually be traced back to:
   a. the government
   b. the person's education
   c. the person's friends
   d. the person's family

7. A low percentage of African American families in America:
   a. have a father at home
   b. have fathers that are poor role models
   c. are led by single mothers
   d. are led by strong fathers

8. The root of African American families' problem is:
   a. perseverance
   b. making unwise choices
   c. slavery
   d. materialism

9. Slavery is the reason why African American families today have so many issues because:
   a. fathers, mothers, and children were sold to different masters, tearing the family apart
   b. family members were afraid to give their hearts to each other because of the pain they could suffer if separated
   c. the social wound it created must be healed
   d. the majority of African American families do not have a strong father in the family

10. Wilson Lynch's strategy of breaking up families resulted in:
    a. slaves having loyalty for their owners only
    b. African American women have had to be both mother and father ever since
    c. African American women have difficulty accepting fathers in their rightful place
    d. fathers are having an easy time accepting their place

True or False:

11. Slavery has affected the ambition and work ethic of African Americans.
12. Cultural wounds cannot be healed without the intervention of the cross.
13. African Americans were not subjected to slavery for the same reason as Israel.
14. African Americans do not have a destiny with God.
15. African Americans are to carry freedom to a new level in America.
16. True freedom contains dignity and honor that God created people to have.

Fill in the blanks:

17. It is by the Lord's ____ that we are ____ and receive ____ for healing in the very place where we are ____.
18. Blacks are going to embrace the ____, receive ___ for their own ____, and start ____ whites with such a ____ that we will all be set ___ by that ____.
19. Uncle Tom of *Uncle Tom's Cabin* truly was a ____ figure as a type of ____. He was more ____ than his owners were and was willing to use his great ____ to lay down his own life to bring about his owners' ____.
20. When African American believers are fully ____, they will bring ____ and true spiritual ____ to the whole ____.
21. The inner cities will become the ____ ____ of God's tabernacle— the place where His ____ and ____ dwells. It will be the greatest ____ of God in ____.

Find the incorrect statement:

22. a. America's makeup of many cultures is why it is so great and why we have great problems.
   b. We have the potential to touch something of the glory of God that few other nations have.
   c. America has the opportunity to overcome and demonstrate the solution to racism.
   d. America, unlike the first Pentecost, will not need to be in one accord to see revival happen.

Find the correct statement:

23. a. Racism will never be defeated on the shores of America.
    b. America can still be the greatest world power in spite of ethnic strife.
    c. If America does not embrace her potential to eliminate racism, she will be destroyed by racism.
    d. Nothing that America can do will be able to defeat the yoke of slavery.

Fill in the chart:

24. Mark whether each statement refers to sheep or goats according to Matthew 25:31-46.

Jesus will separate the nations into	Sheep	Goats
Those who will inherit the Kingdom		
Those who will receive eternal punishment		
Those who will give drink to those who are thirsty		
Those who will not give food to the hungry		
Those who will take strangers in		
Those who will be kind to the least		
Those who will be rejected by the Lord		

25. Why do you think we will we be judged on our oneness with those who are different than ourselves? _____

_____

26. Why do you think the Lord has bestowed His blessings upon America thus far? _____

_____

27. Why is humility key to being open to those who are different from us? _____

_____

Yield

1. Take the goals you have listed in the Apply section and pray over them. Ask the Holy Spirit to strengthen you to the task ahead as you grow in His likeness through these goals.

2. Devote prayer time to any areas the Holy Spirit earmarked as needing prayer. Look up Scriptures that speak to these areas and pray them over your life. Ask someone close to you to pray with you in any area that seems overwhelming to you.

Chapter Three

HEALING CULTURAL WOUNDS

P-R-A-Y
Prepare

1. Get into a framework of spiritual warfare by finding a quiet place to focus your heart with thanksgiving, praise, and worship.
2. Using the title "Healing Cultural Wounds," ask the Lord to give you a humble heart to see what you need to see and hear. Confess anything that comes to mind as you pray.
3. Ask the Holy Spirit to be your Teacher and to help you consider your life in light of His Word as you go through your study time.

Read

1. Read Chapter Three, highlighting important parts that have particular meaning to your life.
2. Make notes of anything you need to apply to your life in the margins.
3. Also, jot down any areas that the Holy Spirit earmarks as needing prayer.

Apply

1. Look over anything you highlighted and reread these sections.
2. Using the notes you made in the margins, make any areas of application into goals by creating a list and a target date of completion.

Goal: Here is a sample: I will help my church overcome spiritual bigotry.
Premise: If our church can celebrate its uniqueness in the Body of Christ, it should celebrate every other church's uniqueness as well.

a. I will ask a leader how I can make a difference in this area, following through on the suggestions given. (7/8)

b. I will spend time in prayer for the next week, asking God to reveal ways in which we can embrace other churches who are different from us without compromising our message. I will write these revelations down and pray over them. (7/15)

c. I will collect newsletters or information on the websites from five other local churches that are different from our church in some obvious way(s) and pray for their success. I will submit my information and prayer to the leader from my church and ask if I can do anything else to help. (7/22)

Goal:

Goal:

3. Answer the questions provided as a means of reviewing the material and creating the repetition necessary to have greater retention and understanding of these principles.

Multiple Choice (there may be more than one correct answer):

1. Cultural sins are passed down from generation to generation until:
   a. people learn how to genetically heal them
   b. we recognize them
   c. we humble ourselves and repent for the sins of the father
   d. Jesus comes again

2. Repentance for the sins of the fathers:
   a. is a new concept to the New Testament Church only
   b. was done by people in the Old Testament who stood in the gap for their people
   c. was created as a pact between God and people
   d. was prayed by Old Testament people who had nothing to do with the sin

3. Standing in the gap for people through prayer is:
   a. the true foundation for the cross
   b. the work of a few radical intercessory types
   c. the true nature of Christ
   d. the same as all other prayer

4. Biblical repentance is:
   a. simply feeling and saying you are sorry
   b. doing good works to make up for the sin
   c. a formula for becoming clean
   d. turning from our evil ways
5. The white church in the South:
   a. tried to remove slavery
   b. set up clear biblical theological discussions against slavery
   c. created a network of help for slaves
   d. gave birth to demented theologies that justified slavery
6. Today, the white church should:
   a. point a finger toward the denominations that perpetuated slavery
   b. lead the battle against the world ruler of racism
   c. forget the past mistakes and move on
   d. destroy the evil that was created against blacks

True or False:

7. The Church must show the world the answer to racism.
8. The Church must first get rid of racism in the world and then it will have the spiritual authority over racism within its walls.
9. The Church is one of the most integrated institutions in the world.
10. The Church has been blessed to miss the sin of spiritual bigotry.
11. Spiritual bigotry is much less prevalent than natural bigotry.
12. Examples of spiritual racism include judging other churches, movements, or people as inferior or frightening because they are not a part of our group.

Fill in the blanks:

13. In Titus 1:8, when Paul listed the qualifications for _____ in the Church, he specified that they be ____. The original Greek states, "one who shows hospitality to _____ or _____."
14. To be a leader of the Church, a believer has to be _____ to those who are _____. This is fundamental to true spiritual _____.
15. One who cannot ____ those who are different is either too ____ or too _____ to be in church _____.

Matching:

16. a. While the world is
degenerating into
increasing ethnic conflicts ____
b. The Church's unity
does not mean that
that ____
c. The Church's unity ____

d. The whole of creation ____

17. a. God desires every church ____

b. The differences in churches
are designed ____
c. The differences in churches
are not designed ____
d. Our insecurity considers
our differences _____

1) reflects the Lord's
love for diversity.

2) is based on the recog-
nition and appreciation
of our differences.

3) we will submit to the
same organizational
structure.

4) the Church will become
increasingly unified.

1) to complement each
other.

2) to be different.

3) to be threats.

4) to create conflict.

Answer the following:

18. Can we expect doctrinal and procedural differences between churches and movements to bring conflict? Why or why not?

_____

_____

19. How will true unity in the Church come? Will we need to compromise our convictions? _____

_____

20. What is behind most church splits? _____

_____

21. How has racism empowered the spirit of death among churches?

_____

_____

22. Describe the barrier between men and women in the world today.

_____

_____

23. Why do men and women need each other's perspectives? _____

_____

_____

24. How can men and women heal the deep wounds within each? ____

_____

_____

Compare/Contrast:

25. How does the Levitical priest's breastplate speak to the way the Church must embrace all groups? _____

_____

26. Compare true unity in the Church to the unity of the world. _____

_____

27. Contrast Jesus' judgment with the world's judgment. _____

_____

Yield

1. Take the goals you have listed in the Apply section and pray over them. Ask the Holy Spirit to strengthen you to the task ahead as you grow in His likeness through these goals.
2. Devote prayer time to any areas the Holy Spirit earmarked as needing prayer. Look up Scriptures that speak to these areas and pray them over your life. Ask someone close to you to pray with you in any area that seems overwhelming to you.

Chapter Four

A PRACTICAL STRATEGY

P-R-A-Y
Prepare

1. Get into a framework of spiritual warfare by finding a quiet place to focus your heart with thanksgiving, praise, and worship.
2. Using the title "A Practical Strategy," ask the Lord to give you a humble heart to see what you need to see and hear. Confess anything that comes to mind as you pray.
3. Ask the Holy Spirit to be your Teacher and to help you consider your life in light of His Word as you go through your study time.

Read

1. Read Chapter Four, highlighting important parts that have particular meaning to your life.
2. Make notes of anything you need to apply to your life in the margins.
3. Also, jot down any areas that the Holy Spirit earmarks as needing prayer.

Apply

1. Look over anything you highlighted and reread these sections.
2. Using the notes you made in the margins, make any areas of application into goals by creating a list and a target date of completion.

Goal: Here is a sample: I will remove the deception of stereotyping people groups through their extreme members or actions. Premise: If I want to have God's perspective toward others, I must learn to lean on Him, rather than on media or hearsay, to understand others.

a. I will use the Internet or library to research a group of people I do not understand. I will take notes in order to have prayer points for this people group. I will learn at least three positive things about them. (4/9)

b. I will take a day to pray for the people group I have researched. Then I will release them to the Kingdom of God. I will ask God to take away the deception from my eyes concerning this group and to open my eyes to the truth. Then I will travail for their sins as well as rejoice for their blessings. (4/12)

c. I will ask the Lord to give me divine encounters with people from my research group so that I can gain divine love for them, even if I disagree with what they represent. (4/16)

Goal:

Goal:

3. Answer the questions provided as a means of reviewing the material and creating the repetition necessary to have greater retention and understanding of these principles.

True or False:

1. In Deuteronomy, the Israelites were commanded to love and teach aliens in their midst.

2. America is the most benevolent power in history, but it is also the most despised on earth.

3. America is known as a country that never offends and insults other cultures.

4. Because we are made up of many cultures, we accept those from other countries and make them feel comfortable here.

5. Churches can reach out to foreigners who are being educated on our college campuses and impact the world.

Matching:

6. a. The ultimate race barrier, with regard to spiritual power _____

   1) is for the sake of the Gospel.

   b. The Jew _____

   2) is the barrier between Jew and Gentile.

c. The reason that Jews have
been hardened ____

3) is the acid test for
our message.

d. Having the Gospel that will
make Jews jealous ____

4) is the embodiment
of the humanistic
spirit.

7. a. The wounds afflicted upon
Jews by the Church ____

1) enable the Lord to extend
grace to us to minister
to Jews.

b. It will take unprecedented
humility on our part to ____

2) overcome racist barriers
against Jews and others.

c. Jews must be grafted into
God's Kingdom so that we ____

3) make our job to reach
them very difficult.

d. We will overcome the spirit
of death and racism when we ____

4) fulfill our
commission.

Fill in the blanks:

8. The Lord dealt with the Jews exclusively for about _____ years.
The time of the Gentiles has now been about _____ years. What we
are coming into now is the time of the ____ and the ____ grafted
into one new ____ through ____.

9. True unity is found in ____, not in ____. When the Church and
Israel are truly ____ together neither will be as they are ___. The
union of the natural and ____ seed of Abraham is required before
the world can see what the true ___ ____ is.

10. In Romans, Paul clearly established God's ____ for Israel and the
Church. He warned against becoming "..._____ toward the [nat-
ural] ____...Do not be conceited, but ____; for if God did not
____ the ____ branches, neither will He ____ _____."

11. For God to reject ____ Israel would be to ____ the very ____ of His
promises made to ____ throughout the entire _____ ____.

12. It will take extraordinary ____ for the Church to fully ___ God's
_____ in ____ Israel, and it will take the same degree of _____ for
____ Israel to see God's ____ in the ____.

Find the incorrect statement:

13. a. Many believe that only converted Jews will be able to reach the Jews.
    b. The Lord sent Peter to the Jews and Paul to the Gentiles to show God's purpose and strategy for winning people.
    c. God should have sent Paul, the Pharisee of Pharisees, to the Jews and Peter, the simple fisherman, to the Gentiles.
    d. Our Gospel is not natural; it is spiritual, and the natural mind still cannot comprehend it.

14. a. The Lord sent Paul to the Gentiles because he was an offense to them.
    b. Paul had to depend upon the Holy Spirit so that he could fulfill his commission.
    c. The only way the Gospel is truly empowered is through the Holy Spirit.
    d. Natural affinities usually help get things out of the way for the Gospel to be preached.

15. a. The Lord humbled the Gentiles by sending them Paul, who was a Jew, and He will humble the Jews by sending them Gentiles.
    b. Jews are the best resources for reaching other Jews for Christ.
    c. The Gentile Church needs to take up the burden of reaching Jews.
    d. The Church desperately needs converted Jews to help us reach other Jews.

Answer the following:

16. How is the news media one of the primary tools being used by the enemy to sow deception and division between peoples? _____

_____

_____

17. Why doesn't "normal" America make the evening news? _____

_____

_____

18. How does the Christian media create an unreal perception of Christianity? _____

_____

19. How do family-oriented sitcoms distort reality? _____

    _____

20. How do the "sound bites" of media affect us? _____

    _____

Multiple Choice (there may be more than one correct answer):

21. Satan has been very successful in causing and maintaining division between people by:
    a. creating ways for us to come together for specific purposes
    b. making strong efforts to speak truth about our shortcomings to others
    c. allowing us to find out for ourselves what is wrong with others
    d. encouraging us to judge other people groups by their most extreme elements

22. The enemy's primary strategy is to have us:
    a. perceive one another through caricatures that have been sown into our minds
    b. make overtures to those who are not like us
    c. bring our enemies to a point of repentance
    d. use Christian love to convince the lost

23. The enemy fears that:
    a. we will remain separate but equal
    b. we can only pretend to be unified
    c. we might come into unity if our perceptions about others come into the truth
    d. we may be able to make headway on our own strength

24. The world tends to view us all according to:
    a. the most extreme elements of the faith
    b. the best of us
    c. the average Christian
    d. the new Christian

25. The enemy's basic strategy is to sow division and misunderstanding by:
    a. showing us the benefits of coming together in unity
    b. having us judge each other after projected images

  c. letting the truth itself divide us

  d. minimizing our differences

26. We must learn to judge other people:

  a. after the Spirit and not after the flesh

  b. only when we can see their faults clearly

  c. so that they will not judge us

  d. not through information from the media but from the Holy Spirit

27. To have a complete picture of what God is doing:

  a. men need women

  b. women need men

  c. blacks need whites

  d. whites need blacks

  e. denominations need each other

28. Love:

  a. can never be fully realized on this earth

  b. is the foundation of all true vision and true prophecy

  c. opens us up to see much more than we could otherwise see

  d. is not the way to be sure people come into unity

Yield

1. Take the goals you have listed in the Apply section and pray over them. Ask the Holy Spirit to strengthen you to the task ahead as you grow in His likeness through these goals.

2. Devote prayer time to any areas the Holy Spirit earmarked as needing prayer. Look up Scriptures that speak to these areas and pray them over your life. Ask someone close to you to pray with you in any area that seems overwhelming to you.

Chapter Five

THE TWO MINISTRIES

P-R-A-Y

Prepare

1. Get into a framework of spiritual warfare by finding a quiet place to focus your heart with thanksgiving, praise, and worship.
2. Using the title "The Two Ministries," ask the Lord to give you a humble heart to see what you need to see and hear. Confess anything that comes to mind as you pray.
3. Ask the Holy Spirit to be your Teacher and to help you consider your life in light of His Word as you go through your study time.

Read

1. Read Chapter Five, highlighting important parts that have particular meaning to your life.
2. Make notes of anything you need to apply to your life in the margins.
3. Also, jot down any areas that the Holy Spirit earmarks as needing prayer.

Apply

1. Look over anything you highlighted and reread these sections.
2. Using the notes you made in the margins, make any areas of application into goals by creating a list and a target date of completion.

Goal: Here is a sample: I will remove insecurity from my life in the area of how others think of me. Premise: If I want to be Christlike toward all people,

I must stop being insecure as this will bring out other sins like being territorial or trying to be superior.

   a. I will research Scriptures on being secure in the Lord and resting on who He says I am in Him. (4/1)
   b. I will make a list of areas that I know make me feel insecure as well as areas where I tend to be judgmental because of my insecurities. (4/3)
   c. I will ask someone to pray with me once a week during the next two months, focusing on my insecurities and possessiveness. I will report to this person changes that I see God making inside of me. (4/12)

Goal:

Goal:

   3. Answer the questions provided as a means of reviewing the material and creating the repetition necessary to have greater retention and understanding of these principles.

Fill in the blanks:

   1. The Scriptures reveal that two acts occur _____ before the throne of God—_____ and _____. The conflict between these two is a focal point of the ____ between the ___ of ____ and the ____ of ____.
   2. Because God has chosen to make the ____ His _____ place, and therefore the place of His ___, it is in the ____ of the ____ that the battle between intercession and accusation now rages.
   3. It is the fundamental nature of Jesus to be an ____, a ____. To the degree that we ___ in Him, Jesus will ___ us to ___. For this reason His Church is called to be a "____ of ___ for __ the ____."
   4. Satan is called "the ___ of our ____…who ___ them before our God ____ and ___." To the degree that the enemy has ____ to our ____, he will use us to ___ and ____ the brethren.
   5. Satan uses the ___, who have ___to the throne, to accomplish the diabolical work of ____ the ____.

Multiple Choice (there may be more than one correct answer):

6. Satan was given the title of "accuser of the brethren" because:
   a. accusation has been his specialty since the Garden of Eden
   b. he stands in Heaven before God accusing them day and night
   c. of his effectiveness in getting brother to turn against brother
   d. he righteously judges our sins

7. When satan turns brother against brother, accusation:
   a. comes because the Holy Spirit is not yet inside of us
   b. destroys the light, the power, and the witness of the Body of Christ
   c. begins because we are helpless to know anything else
   d. makes a pathway to repentance

8. Our ability to accomplish our purpose in this world will be determined by:
   a. the degree to which we can dispel our deadly enemy
   b. the way in which we maneuver through our circumstances
   c. the degree to which we can learn to live for one another
   d. the amount of time we spend being good

9. The unity of the Church:
   a. gives us awesome authority
   b. allows the Father to give us what we ask
   c. is the greatest threat to satan's domain
   d. exponentially multiplies our spiritual authority

10. The access the accuser has to most believers is:
    a. because we are not very intelligent
    b. through their insecurity which makes them territorial or possessive
    c. only closed through making a strong effort to do good works
    d. increased greatly by the authority of influence that one has in the Church

11. If we remove the yoke of criticism from our midst:
    a. we can then live completely perfect lives
    b. we are able to create the means by which we can see God in visions
    c. our light will break out

    d.   our healing will come speedily

    e.   the glory of the Lord will follow us

    f.   the Lord will answer our prayers

    g.   nothing of value will happen

Answer the following:

12. Why is criticism one of the ultimate manifestations of pride?

_____

13. What does pride bring to us?_____

14. What examples of sins has pride caused, as seen in Scripture?

_____

15. Why can't any of us stand at any moment except by the grace of God? _____Why do we need to remind ourselves of that grace when we look at others? _____

Matching:

16. a. When we criticize another
Christian, _____

    b. When we judge one of
God's people _____

    c. When we judge one of
God's leaders _____

    d. When we think we know
best _____

1) we are actually judging God's leadership.

2) we are actually judging God.

3) we are actually saying God does not know what He is doing.

4) we actually say that God's workmanship doesn't meet our standards.

17. a. James 4:11-12 _____

    b. Matthew 7:1-2 _____

    c. Proverbs 18:21 _____

    d. Proverbs 4:18-19

1) Death and life are in the power of the tongue…

2) Do not speak against one another…

3) The path of the just is like the shining sun…

4) Judge not, that you be not judged…

Find the statement that is true:

18. a. Grumbling and complaining really doesn't hurt anyone.
    b. The Israelites grumbled and complained and were justified in doing so.
    c. Grumbling is the chief reason why so many Christians do not walk in the promises of God.
    d. The reason the Israelites did not possess the Promised Land is because the inhabitants were giants.

Find the statement that is false:

19. a. The primary reason for our spiritual health is the way in which we make sure others know their faults.
    b. The primary reason for the darkness, lack of healing, unanswered prayer, and lack of glory is our own critical spirit.
    c. A critical spirit is pointing the finger and speaking wickedness.
    d. Our criticism will bring us to poverty.

Compare/Contrast:

20. Explain the difference between the critical person and the person who humbly accepts others. _____

Answer the following:

21. What does God warn about those who become stumbling blocks?
    _____
22. What instructions do we have to deal with a brother or a sister who is in sin? _____
23. What does having a critical spirit have to do with Jesus rejecting us on Judgment Day? _____
24. Is anyone ever free from following the scriptural precedent for dealing with sin? Explain. _____
25. If we believe a man with a large ministry is in sin and we are unable to persuade him, what are we to do? What are we not to do?_____
26. If we have not followed the Lord's prescribed manner for dealing with a brother in sin, what then are our limits? _____
    _____

27. What are some of the excuses for talking about someone else's sin?

_____

Yield

1. Take the goals you have listed in the Apply section and pray over them. Ask the Holy Spirit to strengthen you to the task ahead as you grow in His likeness through these goals.
2. Devote prayer time to any areas the Holy Spirit earmarked as needing prayer. Look up Scriptures that speak to these areas and pray them over your life. Ask someone close to you to pray with you in any area that seems overwhelming to you.

Chapter Six

LOVE AND VISION

P-R-A-Y
Prepare

1. Get into a framework of spiritual warfare by finding a quiet place to focus your heart with thanksgiving, praise, and worship.
2. Using the title "Love and Vision," ask the Lord to give you a humble heart to see what you need to see and hear. Confess anything that comes to mind as you pray.
3. Ask the Holy Spirit to be your Teacher and to help you consider your life in light of His Word as you go through your study time.

Read

1. Read Chapter Six, highlighting important parts that have particular meaning to your life.
2. Make notes of anything you need to apply to your life in the margins.
3. Also, jot down any areas that the Holy Spirit earmarks as needing prayer.

Apply

1. Look over anything you highlighted and reread these sections.
2. Using the notes you made in the margins, make any areas of application into goals by creating a list and a target date of completion.

Goal: Here is a sample: I will become more loving toward someone who particularly rubs me the wrong way. Premise: If I want to be able to walk uprightly, I must be able to develop the love of God in my heart where I don't have it so that I can be able to accurately discern truth.

    a.   I will choose a person that will test my ability to love. (1/9)

    b.   I will pray for this person daily for 30 days, asking God to help me love them as He does. (1/15)

    c.   I will read Scriptures that speak about loving the outcast or my enemies so I can put His Word in my heart to help me love in ways I have not done thus far. (1/26)

Goal:

Goal:

3.   Answer the questions provided as a means of reviewing the material and creating the repetition necessary to have greater retention and understanding of these principles.

Answer the following:

1.   When we become challenged with someone else's (presumed) sin, what do we need to remember from Scripture? _____

_____

2.   Does the Lord deal with all of our sins at the same time? Explain.

_____

_____

3.   Why was Matthew 18 written? How can we abuse this Scripture?

_____

_____

4.   How did Christ correct the churches listed in the book of Revelation? How is this a model for us? _____

_____

_____

5.   How does satan try to bring correction to the Church? _____

_____

_____

6.   Fill in the chart:

Scripture	Key Words	Instruction for Our Discernment
1 Corinthians 5:12	Within the Church	Criticism can be rooted in true discernment
Proverbs 6:12-15		
James 3:13-18		
Matthew 5:21-26		
1 John 4:20		
1 John 3:15-16		

True or False:

7. People we criticize may truly be in error.

8. When we discern sin, we must then choose whether we are going to accuse or intercede.

9. How we deal with discernment cannot determine the outcome of our own spiritual lives.

10. We can mask our suspicious nature by calling it "discernment."

11. True wisdom is found when we logically see all sides and come to a conclusion based on that logic.

12. We can reap differently from what we sow in terms of giving grace and mercy.

13. Slander is not considered a top sin that will affect our worship of God.

14. We cannot pay our way out of speaking wrongly against someone else.

15. When the Lord judges someone as sheep, they have shown themselves to be 100 percent pure in everything they have done.

16. When the Lord judges someone as a goat, they have shown themselves to be unfaithful in everything on earth.

17. Jesus loved even those friends who deserted Him and denied Him.

Fill in the blanks:

18. One of the great tragedies of Church history has been the way _____ of each move of God have become ___ and _____ of succeeding moves.

19. Numerous leaders have spent their lives _____ _____ only to finish as _____ for the _____, who makes them a ___ ____ for the next move.

20. We might think and say we would ____ oppose a move of God, but that is what previous church _____ had thought and said as well. We must be careful or we will find ourselves _____ of these actions because of ____.

21. Each new move of God has resulted in the ___ of more ___ to the Church. This light is not ___ truth, but truth that was ___ to the Church through the Dark Ages of her history.

22. The basic reason we oppose the new move of God is mostly due to _____. Those who have been ___ to the light that they have had for a ____ have difficulty believing that anyone is more ____, or that the Lord would want to ____ anyone but them for further ____of His ____ and ____.

23. The only remedy that will keep leaders from ultimately falling into the trap of opposing new moves of God is to seek the ___ and ___ of John the Baptist. Just as John ____ the way for Jesus and it was his greatest ___ to see Jesus go ___ than he did, so we need to release others to surpass us.

24. The pride of thinking we are ___ than those who went before us can ____ us from going any ____ ourselves. The only command with a promise is that which ____ us to ____ our fathers and mothers,

referring to ____ and ____ fathers and mothers. Our spiritual ____ is directly related to this issue.

25. To fail to honor those who have been our spiritual predecessors is to ___ ourselves from the __ and ____ that enables us to receive spiritual ____.

Yield

1. Take the goals you have listed in the Apply section and pray over them. Ask the Holy Spirit to strengthen you to the task ahead as you grow in His likeness through these goals.

2. Devote prayer time to any areas the Holy Spirit earmarked as needing prayer. Look up Scriptures that speak to these areas and pray them over your life. Ask someone close to you to pray with you in any area that seems overwhelming to you.

Chapter Seven

THE HEART OF THE FREEDOM FIGHTER

P-R-A-Y
Prepare

1. Get into a framework of spiritual warfare by finding a quiet place to focus your heart with thanksgiving, praise, and worship.
2. Using the title "The Heart of the Freedom Fighter," ask the Lord to give you a humble heart to see what you need to see and hear. Confess anything that comes to mind as you pray.
3. Ask the Holy Spirit to be your Teacher and to help you consider your life in light of His Word as you go through your study time.

Read

1. Read Chapter Seven, highlighting important parts that have particular meaning to your life.
2. Make notes of anything you need to apply to your life in the margins.
3. Also, jot down any areas that the Holy Spirit earmarks as needing prayer.

Apply

1. Look over anything you highlighted and reread these sections.
2. Using the notes you made in the margins, make any areas of application into goals by creating a list and a target date of completion.

Goal:

Goal:

Goal:

3. Answer the questions provided as a means of reviewing the material and creating the repetition necessary to have greater retention and understanding of these principles.

Answer the following:

1. In order for the Church to advance, what must future leaders become? What does this mean? _____

   _____

2. According to Philippians 2:3-9, what must our character be like if we are to have spiritual leadership? _____

3. According to Luke 14:11, what is the maxim that we are to live by? How does this work? _____

   _____

4. According to James 4:10, where should we humble ourselves? Why? _____

5. According to First Peter 5:6, under whom should we humble ourselves? Why? _____

6. How have the evil spirits of self-promotion and territorial preservation hurt Church leadership? _____

7. How can the older generation hurt the new generation from moving forward in Kingdom work? How can the younger generation hurt the older generation? _____

   _____

8. Using Jesus' relationship with John the Baptist, analyze what we must do to be sure we promote the move of God. How did John honor and support the new ministry that Jesus brought? How did Jesus honor and submit to John's ministry? _____

   _____

   _____

True or False:

9. The new generation of Church leadership must submit to those who have gone before them if they are to fulfill all righteousness.

10. When a new generation of spiritual leadership emerges, the older generation can continue to have prominence.

11. The new generation of Church leadership should always honor those who went before them, or they will be in jeopardy of disqualifying themselves from advancing the Kingdom.

12. The arrogance of the new order is not an affront to the Spirit of God.

13. The old order that resists God in new things which He begins to do is an affront to the Spirit.

Multiple Choice (there may be more than one correct answer):

14. Many accused saints:
   a. eventually become saints who stop others from accusing
   b. become accusers themselves
   c. always see justice done on earth
   d. become reactionary, which leads to bitterness

15. The only things that can break the cycle of the accused becoming the accuser is:
   a. forgiveness
   b. judgment
   c. personality studies
   d. humility

16. The sins of the parents will become the sins of the children until we:
   a. pull ourselves up in our strength
   b. make a pact with those who sin like us to correct them
   c. receive the grace of the cross
   d. go before a leadership council to rectify the situations

17. God gives grace to:
   a. the proud
   b. the arrogant
   c. the humble
   d. the self-absorbed

18. We should pray that we would be forgiven:
    a. for the sins of the fathers
    b. even though we did nothing wrong ever
    c. but not follow through to walk in obedience
    d. and make it known that we now walk in purity

Fill in the blanks:

19. There will be a spiritual generation that will be _____ just as every one before it, however, they will not go on to _____ the next generation. They will not be subject to the "_____ of _____," assuming that all things will be _____ with them.

20. Those of this generation will find the _____ of the _____ and will forgive from the ___ those who _____ them.

21. They will perceive and even _____ that their children, _____ and natural, may go ___ in Christ than they did, and they will ___ in it.

22. They will give their _____ to making the way of the ___ generation as _____ as _____, and then they will _____ to _____ as that generation _____.

23. This will be the generation of the ___ of Elijah who will ___ the hearts of the _____ to the _____, and the hearts of the _____ to the _____.

24. Our ability to be the generation that _____ the way for the Lord and His _____ _____ will be determined by which of the two _____ we become a part of—_____ or _____.

25. Let us now remove the terrible yoke of "_____ the _____" from our midst and begin turning our _____ into _____.

26. According to Isaiah 58:8-9;11-12, the _____ spirit is the reason why there is so little _____, _____, ___ _____, or the _____ of the Lord _____.

27. If we turn our criticisms into _____, we will be those who _____ the age-old _____, and repair the _____ between God and ___, and therefore between people and other ___.

Yield

1. Take the goals you have listed in the Apply section and pray over them. Ask the Holy Spirit to strengthen you to the task ahead as you grow in His likeness through these goals.

2. Devote prayer time to any areas the Holy Spirit earmarked as needing prayer. Look up Scriptures that speak to these areas and pray them over your life. Ask someone close to you to pray with you in any area that seems overwhelming to you.

Part II

THE STRONGHOLD
OF WITCHCRAFT

Chapter Eight

Understanding Witchcraft

P-R-A-Y

Prepare

1. Get into a framework of spiritual warfare by finding a quiet place to focus your heart with thanksgiving, praise, and worship.
2. Using the title "Understanding Witchcraft," ask the Lord to give you a humble heart to see what you need to see and hear. Confess anything that comes to mind as you pray.
3. Ask the Holy Spirit to be your Teacher and to help you consider your life in light of His Word as you go through your study time.

Read

1. Read Chapter Eight, highlighting important parts that have particular meaning to your life.
2. Make notes of anything you need to apply to your life in the margins.
3. Also, jot down any areas that the Holy Spirit earmarks as needing prayer.

Apply

1. Look over anything you highlighted and reread these sections.
2. Using the notes you made in the margins, make any areas of application into goals by creating a list and a target date of completion.

Goal:

Goal:

Goal:

3. Answer the questions provided as a means of reviewing the material and creating the repetition necessary to have greater retention and understanding of these principles.

Fill in the blanks:

1. One of the goals of many involved in witchcraft is to destroy ____. Many Christians are presently suffering some form of ____ from those who practice ____. Discerning the ____ of these attacks, and knowing how to ____ them is becoming ____ for ____ believers.
2. The only way a Christian can be defeated by witchcraft is through our own ____ or ____. As we maintain our ____ in Christ, taking on the ___ ___ of God and remaining ____, we will not only ___, but will ____ against any attack from hell.
3. Witchcraft is ____ ____ authority; it is using a spirit ____ than the Holy Spirit to ____. ____, or ____ others. Though witchcraft has its origin in the ____ ____ of man, it usually degenerates quickly into ____ power.
4. Witchcraft includes using emotional ____ to ____ others and using ____ or soul ____ to enlist ____, even for the work of ___. Businessmen can use witchcraft when they ___ to find ___ ____ while pursuing a deal. Salesmen can use marketing techniques that are ____ tactics which are a form of witchcraft.
5. The primary defense against counterfeit spiritual authority is to ___ in ____ ____. Establishing our lives on ____ and ____ in the ____ to accomplish what ____ us are essential ____ to becoming ___ from the ____ and ____ of witchcraft.
6. David established a position of ____ ____ authority that would ultimately be ____ in the ___ of God. He did this by refusing to take ____ or seek ___. Instead David completely ___ in God to ___ him in the position that He had ___ for him.

7. Any authority or _____ that we gain by our own_____ or _____ will become a _____ _____ to us and will hinder our ability to receive __ ___ from God. If we want to walk in _____ spiritual authority like David, we will have to _____ _____ in the Lord to establish us in ___ ___.

True or False:

8. Being established in true spiritual authority is a fortress that simply cannot be penetrated by the enemy.
9. When we establish ourselves in a position of authority, we will have great peace.
10. The first principle of being delivered from witchcraft is to repent of all the ways that we have used it ourselves in our own lives and ministries.
11. What God is building is raised up by might and power.
12. When we build on something other than the Spirit of God, it can still have great benefits to the Kingdom.
13. The flesh wars against the Spirit, regardless of how good we try to make the flesh look.
14. The Lord helps us overcome our tendency to use manipulative tactics by allowing us to endure rejection.

Matching:

15. a. Because rejection can be such a difficult task _____
    b. Rejection drives us to _____

    c. Learning to pray for our persecutors is essential _____
    d. We must come into the level of maturity where _____

1) retaliate or try to prove ourselves.
2) if we are to exercise true spiritual authority.
3) the love of Christ controls us.
4) it can also be a great opportunity to be delivered from the fear of man.

16. a. Our ability to walk in true spiritual authority will _____
    b. Rejection provides an opportunity for us to _____

1) lead to witchcraft.
2) be destroyed by self-seeking, self-promotion, or self-preservation.

c. We must embrace rejection as ____ 3) a discipline of the Lord.

d. Not embracing rejection as the Lord's discipline may ____ 4) grow in grace and die a little more to ambition and pride.

17. a. Because witchcraft is basically rooted in the fear of man ____ 1) the paranoia of those who are trapped grows.

b. Those who are caught in the deadly trap of the fear of man ____ 2) the void will be filled by the counterfeit of witchcraft.

c. As manipulation and control spirits increase their dominion ____ 3) will fear those who walk in the true anointing and authority.

d. When one in spiritual authority rebels against the Holy Spirit ____ 4) people who operate in witchcraft are trapped.

18. a. Spiritual authority ____ 1) seek a position of authority.

b. If we are wise, we will not ____ 2) be given authority over kingdoms.

c. Satan tempts everyone to bow to him and ____ 3) servants of all.

d. God calls us to rule over kingdoms by becoming ____ 4) is a dangerous occupation.

Multiple Choice (there may be more than one correct answer):

19. The higher the position of authority:
    a. the more benefits you receive
    b. the easier things become
    c. the more dangerous it is
    d. the more people are affected by even seemingly insignificant decisions

20. True spiritual authority is:
    a. a burden to be carried
    b. not an honor to be sought
    c. to be sought after
    d. earned through good works

21. Someone called to a position of leadership in the Church:
    a. can direct people any way they think is right
    b. must have the devotion of David
    c. should be prepared to receive grace
    d. should be careful not to let presumption kill their leadership
    e. should seek words of wisdom even more than words of knowledge
22. Those who attain prominence before humility:
    a. will almost certainly fall
    b. must follow the path of loneliness
    c. can never become humble
    d. are not operating on the grace of God
23. Those in church leadership:
    a. must recognize their great wealth of knowledge
    b. must be wary of using witchcraft
    c. must be aware they will be a primary target of those who use witchcraft
    d. must be careful of those who have fallen into subtle forms of manipulation to gain influence

Answer the following:

24. What is white witchcraft within the Church? _____
    _____

25. How is Jezebel from Scripture an archetype of witchcraft? _____
    _____

26. Even though we understand we have more power than satan, how can we still be overcome by evil? _____

27. What is our first defense against the enemy through witchcraft or any other tactic? _____

Yield

1. Take the goals you have listed in the Apply section and pray over them. Ask the Holy Spirit to strengthen you to the task ahead as you grow in His likeness through these goals.
2. Devote prayer time to any areas the Holy Spirit earmarked as needing prayer. Look up Scriptures that speak to these areas and pray

them over your life. Ask someone close to you to pray with you in any area that seems overwhelming to you.

Chapter Nine

THE STINGS OF WITCHCRAFT

P-R-A-Y
Prepare

1. Get into a framework of spiritual warfare by finding a quiet place to focus your heart with thanksgiving, praise, and worship.
2. Using the title "The Stings of Witchcraft," ask the Lord to give you a humble heart to see what you need to see and hear. Confess anything that comes to mind as you pray.
3. Ask the Holy Spirit to be your Teacher and to help you consider your life in light of His Word as you go through your study time.

Read

1. Read Chapter Nine, highlighting important parts that have particular meaning to your life.
2. Make notes of anything you need to apply to your life in the margins.
3. Also, jot down any areas that the Holy Spirit earmarks as needing prayer.

Apply

1. Look over anything you highlighted and reread these sections.
2. Using the notes you made in the margins, make any areas of application into goals by creating a list and a target date of completion.

Goal:

Goal:

Goal:

3. Answer the questions provided as a means of reviewing the material and creating the repetition necessary to have greater retention and understanding of these principles.

Answer the following:

1. How do the attacks of witchcraft usually work? How does the series of attacks overwhelm people? _____

2. What are the eight successive stings that witchcraft usually produces? Have you ever seen this progression in your own life or in the life of someone else? In your own words, define each one.

_____

_____

3. How does the process of witchcraft work to make it difficult to discern? _____

4. What are some of the sources of witchcraft that are less obvious to Christians? Have you ever been attacked by any of these sources? Was it easy or difficult for you to identify the attack? _____

_____

5. How can prayer be used by those who are practicing white witchcraft? _____

6. What are some of the sources of charismatic witchcraft? _____

7. Even when we recognize attacks and stand against them, how can we still be defeated? _____

8. What do we need to do to be sure we respond to attacks in the right way? _____

9. How can we begin to free ourselves from the power of witchcraft? _____

10. What is the nature of our battle? What are our weapons? _____

Fill in the chart:

11. Add the stings of witchcraft.

Progression	Sting	Source Notes
1	Discouragement	No apparent reason Difficulties seem insurmountable Want to give up even though things haven't become worse
2		
3		
4		
5		
6		
7		
8		

True or False:

12. In Scripture, the Amalekites typified the people of Israel and God.
13. The Amalekites typically attacked the weak and defenseless.

14. Through witchcraft, the enemy seeks to weaken believers so that they will begin to fall behind and become easy prey.
15. Israel was warned to defeat the Amalekites and take prisoners and spoil from them.
16. We have a perpetual war with satan, and we cannot take any prisoners.
17. We can use what was satan's and redeem it for use for the service of God.
18. There can be no alliance with the enemy. If we do not fight we will be pinned.
19. Christians who do not recognize witchcraft within the Church can be defeated, losing their vision, their ministries, their families, and even their lives.

Fill in the blank:

20. If we do not obey the Lord and utterly ___ the enemy we ____, he will eventually ____ us off.
21. We cannot be foolish enough to think that we can ___ the enemy as our ___; in his ___, he will quickly ___ the ____.
22. In _____ 6:12, Paul says that we do not wrestle against ___ and ___, but against ____ and ____.
23. We have no option as to whether or not we are going to do ____ _____—if we want to ____, we must ____.

Yield

1. Take the goals you have listed in the Apply section and pray over them. Ask the Holy Spirit to strengthen you to the task ahead as you grow in His likeness through these goals.
2. Devote prayer time to any areas the Holy Spirit earmarked as needing prayer. Look up Scriptures that speak to these areas and pray them over your life. Ask someone close to you to pray with you in any area that seems overwhelming to you.

Chapter Ten

Victory Over Witchcraft

P-R-A-Y
Prepare

1. Get into a framework of spiritual warfare by finding a quiet place to focus your heart with thanksgiving, praise, and worship.
2. Using the title "Victory Over Witchcraft," ask the Lord to give you a humble heart to see what you need to see and hear. Confess anything that comes to mind as you pray.
3. Ask the Holy Spirit to be your Teacher and to help you consider your life in light of His Word as you go through your study time.

Read

1. Read Chapter Ten, highlighting important parts that have particular meaning to your life.
2. Make notes of anything you need to apply to your life in the margins.
3. Also, jot down any areas that the Holy Spirit earmarks as needing prayer.

Apply

1. Look over anything you highlighted and reread these sections.
2. Using the notes you made in the margins, make any areas of application into goals by creating a list and a target date of completion.

Goal:

Goal:

Goal:

3. Answer the questions provided as a means of reviewing the material and creating the repetition necessary to have greater retention and understanding of these principles.

Answer the following:

1. According to Revelation 12:11, how do we overcome satan? Explain these three in detail. _____

_____

2. Explain how self-centeredness makes us vulnerable to satan's attack in our lives. _____

3. When we reckon ourselves dead to this world, how does the enemy's access to us cease? _____

4. Why are all three elements from Revelation 12:11 necessary for complete victory? _____

5. Is victory possible for the Church? How do we know? _____

6. What does Isaiah 14:16-17 tell us about our reaction to seeing satan? _____

7. What does Isaiah 60:1-2 tell us about what will happen when darkness covers the earth? _____

8. What is our mandate for combating satan and witchcraft? _____

Matching:

9. Match the Scripture reference with the attack of witchcraft that it addresses.

   a. James 3:17 _____   1) Overcoming
                                    Discouragement

   b. 1 Cor. 14:33 _____   2) Overcoming Despair
   c. Gen. 4:6-7 _____   3) Overcoming
                                    Depression

   d. 2 Cor. 1:8-9 _____   4) Overcoming Confusion

Fill in the Chart:

10.

Overcoming	Principles to Remember	Personal Notes
Discouragement	God does not author discourage-ment; He authors faith He is the source of hope, not disap-pointment His correction is peaceable and gentle	I need to reject discourage-ment quickly and instinctively I must not let discourage-ment dictate my course I must keep my shield of faith up
Confusion		

Yield

1. Take the goals you have listed in the Apply section and pray over them. Ask the Holy Spirit to strengthen you to the task ahead as you grow in His likeness through these goals.

2. Devote prayer time to any areas the Holy Spirit earmarked as needing prayer. Look up Scriptures that speak to these areas and pray
   them over your life. Ask someone close to you to pray with you in
   any area that seems overwhelming to you.

Chapter Eleven

COMBATING NEW AGE WITCHCRAFT

P-R-A-Y
Prepare

1. Get into a framework of spiritual warfare by finding a quiet place to focus your heart with thanksgiving, praise, and worship.
2. Using the title "Combating New Age Witchcraft," ask the Lord to give you a humble heart to see what you need to see and hear. Confess anything that comes to mind as you pray.
3. Ask the Holy Spirit to be your Teacher and to help you consider your life in light of His Word as you go through your study time.

Read

1. Read Chapter Eleven, highlighting important parts that have particular meaning to your life.
2. Make notes of anything you need to apply to your life in the margins.
3. Also, jot down any areas that the Holy Spirit earmarks as needing prayer.

Apply

1. Look over anything you highlighted and reread these sections.
2. Using the notes you made in the margins, make any areas of application into goals by creating a list and a target date of completion.

Goal:

Goal:

Goal:

3. Answer the questions provided as a means of reviewing the material and creating the repetition necessary to have greater retention and understanding of these principles.

Fill in the blanks:

1. The New Age movement is basically a combination of _____ and _____, disguised to make it _____ to ____ _____ professionals. These professionals are not only the most _____, they are also the ____ and most _____. They are also a group that the Church has become increasingly ____ in reaching.

2. Information is now the most ____ ____ in the world, and the job of ___, ____, ____, and ____ knowledge has become the world's ____ industry. Daniel 12:4 predicted that "_____ **will increase.**" Few have comprehended the ___ to which this would happen.

3. Because people were created to have _____ with God, who is Spirit, there is a ____ ____ in each person that hungers for the _____. The day of supernatural _____ is over. Those who do not know the true ____ ____ of God will become increasingly subject to the ___ and ____ _____ _____ of the enemy.

4. **"For the kingdom of God does not consist in ___ but in ____"** (1 Cor. 4:20). Satan is quite content to fight the battle on the level of ____ and ____. Satan will have little problem _____ us if we do not know the ___ of God, which is a ____ _____ of God's Kingdom.

5. Those who really believe the Bible will walk in ___. Righteousness is the result of ____ in our ____, not just our ___, and those who do not know the __ of God are only ____ in Him in their ____.

6. Considering the foolish antics of some movements, it is easy to understand why many shy away from the ___ of the ___. But this too is one of the ___ that ___ the true ___ from those who only

know ___ and ___—God has made the ___ things of the world to confound the ___.

Matching:

7. a. Churches that have rejected the supernatural power of God ____

    1) magnifies the people's hunger for the supernatural.

    b. The battle for people's souls ____

    2) have become increasingly irrelevant.

    c. The more secularized society becomes, the more it actually ____

    3) deceived into thinking are powers resident within people.

    d. Atheists tend to be drawn to the basest forms of witchcraft, which they are ____

    4) is intensely supernatural in nature.

Multiple Choice (there may be more than one correct answer):

8. The denominations and movements within the Church that have rejected the power of God:
    a. are growing at an incredible rate
    b. have become irrelevant and boring
    c. have little or no power to attract converts
    d. have been strong to reject influences from the New Age movement
    e. are tolerating the perverted and receiving them and unbelievers as members
    f. are refusing to ordain the perverted as pastors and leaders
9. The conflict between the Kingdom of God and the kingdom of evil:
    a. is only in the minds of conservative believers
    b. has already been lost to the prince of the air
    c. is not just a conflict between truth and error
    d. is a confrontation of supernatural powers seeking to fill the spiritual void in man
10. True Christianity:
    a. is not just a matter of words
    b. does not acknowledge the supernatural power of God

    c. is a demonstration of God's love and power to save, heal, and deliver

    d. makes no claim to the spiritual gifts

11. To overcome the increasing power of the enemy we must:

    a. ignore what he does and it will go away

    b. keep on using our will to overcome him

    c. create time for us to make new weapons against him

    d. desire earnestly spiritual gifts

    e. know the true power of God

Answer the following:

12. Is it enough to be open to spiritual gifts? Why or why not? _____

_____

13. Is it biblical to seek the Giver and not the gifts? Explain your answer. _____

14. Why do all believers long in their hearts for the supernatural, whether they know it or not? _____

15. What is "true Christianity" comprised of? How did Jesus demonstrate this? _____

16. How does our spiritual void come into play with witchcraft? _____

_____

Matching:

17. a. Spiritual gifts available to the Church ____

    b. Those who avoid spiritual gifts ____

    c. We must walk by faith, not fear if we ____

    d. Fear will lead to deception if we ____

18. a. If we are going to fulfill the purposes of God ____

1) are certain to be deceived by counterfeit gifts.

2) are allowing it to be our motivation.

3) are being counterfeited by the enemy.

4) are to stay on the path that leads to life.

1) what we see with eyes of our hearts will be more real than what we see with our natural eyes.

b. If we are going to walk in
the power of God ____

2) because it takes faith
to reach beyond the
natural realm to the
supernatural God.

c. Faith is the door to fellowship
with God ____

3) we must have more
faith in God's ability
to lead us into truth
than we do in the
enemy's ability to
deceive us.

d. As we walk in faith ____

4) it will take faith willing to risk leaving
everything behind to
seek what He is building.

19. a. When we walk in faith ____

1) we start to see the Lord
so clearly, we serve
Him more than
anything else.

b. Those who walk in faith
are naturally ____

2) we begin living more
for the eternal than
the temporal.

c. We take a major step toward
being delivered from
witchcraft when ____

3) almost always become
darkened and evil in
nature themselves.

d. Those who give themselves to
becoming authorities on the
nature of evil ____

4) going to appear foolish
to those who are of
a "natural mind."

20. a. We do not need to study the
darkness as much as we ____

1) will overpower the
evil supernatural power.

b. Light ____

2) need to study the light.

c. If we walk in the true supernatural power of God we ____

3) will always over-
power darkness.

d. Without the power of God ____

4) the increasing power of
the enemy will not be
effectively confronted.

True or False:

21. Most cults and New Age groups are now blatantly attacking Christianity, focusing on the Church as the main target of their sorcery.
22. Those who use witchcraft are not only infiltrating the Church, they are using their power to cast spells on those in ministry.
23. The solution for those churches that are under attack from witchcraft is to know and walk in the might of themselves.
24. As the Church grows in true spiritual authority, the cults will gain in strength against us.
25. When combating evil powers, we must fight on satan's terms.
26. Blessings are more powerful than any curses and will quickly overcome them.
27. Many of the "yokes" and human expectations that we face have some power of manipulation and witchcraft attached to them.
28. When the Lord puts a yoke on us, it can be quite difficult and heavy.
29. When we bless those who curse us or use witchcraft, we do not bless what they are doing, but we pray they will be delivered.

Yield

1. Take the goals you have listed in the Apply section and pray over them. Ask the Holy Spirit to strengthen you to the task ahead as you grow in His likeness through these goals.
2. Devote prayer time to any areas the Holy Spirit earmarked as needing prayer. Look up Scriptures that speak to these areas and pray them over your life. Ask someone close to you to pray with you in any area that seems overwhelming to you.

Chapter Twelve

WITCHCRAFT IN THE MEDIA

P-R-A-Y
Prepare

1. Get into a framework of spiritual warfare by finding a quiet place to focus your heart with thanksgiving, praise, and worship.
2. Using the title "Witchcraft in the Media," ask the Lord to give you a humble heart to see what you need to see and hear. Confess anything that comes to mind as you pray.
3. Ask the Holy Spirit to be your Teacher and to help you consider your life in light of His Word as you go through your study time.

Read

1. Read Chapter Twelve, highlighting important parts that have particular meaning to your life.
2. Make notes of anything you need to apply to your life in the margins.
3. Also, jot down any areas that the Holy Spirit earmarks as needing prayer.

Apply

1. Look over anything you highlighted and reread these sections.
2. Using the notes you made in the margins, make any areas of application into goals by creating a list and a target date of completion.

Goal:

Goal:

Goal:

3. Answer the questions provided as a means of reviewing the material and creating the repetition necessary to have greater retention and understanding of these principles.

Select the statement that is not true:

1. a. Peter wrote that we should be **"looking for and hastening the coming of the day of God…"**
    b. If we can hasten the coming of the day of God, we can also delay it.
    c. The enemy knows his time is short.
    d. The enemy wants to hasten the day of the Lord so he can accuse us.

2. a. We must address major stumbling blocks to spiritual advancement to receive the full benefit of the impending awakening.
    b. The harvest is basically just a great revival.
    c. The harvest will bring reaping of everything sown, both good and evil.
    d. The tares will be taken out first which will cause pain for a season.

3. a. Televangelists who have been involved in scandals are examples of tares.
    b. The scandals of televangelists have uprooted erroneous practices and theologies in the Church.
    c. The tares should have been exposed by the Church but were instead exposed by the media.
    d. The Lord is using the secular media to discipline the Church.

4. a. Much of the Church has given herself to repentance.
    b. Our sovereignty will be restored when our repentance is genuine enough to be acceptable to God.
    c. Heathen nations and the secular media have become more acceptable to God, so He has used them against us.

d. Our sovereignty will be restored when the Church is able to judge herself.

5.
  a. Journalism has become one of the primary platforms of the enemy.

  b. Foundational principles of modern journalism have married it more to Greek philosophy than to Christianity.

  c. Most Christian journalists do not operate according to Greek philosophy.

  d. The Christian media has at times proven less honorable and truthful than the secular media.

6.
  a. The Christian media is now founded more upon a humanistic philosophy than biblical principles.

  b. The Christian media is one of the greatest sources of deadly poison, through the spirit of unrighteous judgment, that is spreading in the Western Church.

  c. The Lord may have used the media to judge us because they are listening to Him more than us.

  d. We should not take on the way of the heathen, but return to God's righteous judgment as outlined in His Word.

True or False:

7. There is a kind of healthy skepticism that wants to believe.

8. There is a kind of healthy skepticism that wants to doubt.

9. Criticism has an appearance of wisdom but it is the fruit of the Tree of Knowledge of Good and Evil.

10. Journalists are at least fair to not criticize when they are writing an article about a church.

11. When journalists pass on gossip, they are not responsible for the gossip as they are just quoting it.

12. When journalists expose dirt in the name of "protecting" people, they are actually throwing stumbling blocks in their way.

13. Ephesians 4:29 tells us to be careful to not let any unwholesome word proceed from our mouths. We are only to speak words for edification.

Fill in the blanks:

14. The Lord appoints ___ in the Church to give it both ____ and ____. The Lord sets high ___ for those elders who would be given such ____. Journalists need to have the same accountability and be held to ___ ____.

15. Christian journalists must be careful not to ____ public opinion and dictate ____. The ability to articulate does not give the right to exert ___ ____ in the Church.

16. Christian journalists must adhere to the same biblical ___ for leadership in the Church as appointed ___ do. Some journalists have obvious spiritual ____ as teachers, pastors, etc. When they are faithful to biblical ____, they can exercise the ____ they have been given by God through their writing. But they can become ____ ____ if they do not comply with biblical ____.

17. Humanistic philosophy of journalism has the appearance of ___ and the search for ___, but it is actually in conflict with the ___ ____. If we're going to be "created in ___ and ____ of the ___," we must put on a new ___, and live by a different ___ than that of the ___.

Multiple Choice (there may be more than one correct answer):

18. The accuracy of reporting in Christian journalism:
    a. is better than most
    b. has not proven to be any higher than in secular journalism
    c. has more of a "spiritual" slant to the reporting than secular media
    d. cannot be better than secular reporting because the sources are the same

19. Much of the investigative reporting of Christian journalists is:
    a. shockingly dishonest and untrue
    b. prone to gossip, hearsay, or apparent imagination
    c. incorrect because of the flawed research
    d. falls to the lowest levels of even the world's standards

20. The media of today:
    a. may hurt someone due to malice but not due to carelessness
    b. is not intoxicated with its own power and influence

c. needs to consider what people will say about them rather than what God will say

d. finds truth and reports on this only

e. one of the above

21. Television ministries:

a. have come under severe judgment in the last few years

b. are for the most part evil

c. have often given more influence to people in the Church than God ever intended them to have

d. have lost the trust and esteem of many in America

22. The Christian media:

a. is about to be exonerated for everything of which they have been accused

b. must bear the judgment of their profession

c. will come under scrutiny and intense pressure

d. are to be applauded for their integrity and truth

e. will receive the same measure of judgment that they measured out to others

23. Judgment against the Christian media:

a. is inevitable, no matter what is done to rectify it at this point

b. can be avoided by genuine repentance

c. will not be meted out because of their good intentions

d. will come because of their unrighteous judgments

24. The difference between the Christian journalists today and the writings of correction within the New Testament is:

a. that the New Testament occurred in a different time and with different issues

b. that the writers of today's Christian journalism are not good writers

c. the writers of the New Testament had the authority to correct those to whom they wrote

d. most correction in Christian journalism is based on courage and not authority

25. The Church is full of unrighteous judgment because:

a. there is no format for righteous judgment

b. elders have not taken their proper places at the gates

    c.   division is sown by hearsay and bad reporting in the Christian media

    d.   sin is exposed by those who do not help to rectify the errors

26. We will continue to be subject to the unrighteous judgment of the world because:

    a.   we are incompetent judges

    b.   we are neglectful of the mandate to provide righteous judgment

    c.   no one has thought of us as a holy people

    d.   we are incapable of perfection

Yield

1. Take the goals you have listed in the Apply section and pray over them. Ask the Holy Spirit to strengthen you to the task ahead as you grow in His likeness through these goals.

2. Devote prayer time to any areas the Holy Spirit earmarked as needing prayer. Look up Scriptures that speak to these areas and pray them over your life. Ask someone close to you to pray with you in any area that seems overwhelming to you.

Part III

THE RELIGIOUS SPIRIT

Chapter Thirteen

UNDERSTANDING THE RELIGIOUS SPIRIT

P-R-A-Y
Prepare

1. Get into a framework of spiritual warfare by finding a quiet place to focus your heart with thanksgiving, praise, and worship.
2. Using the title "Understanding the Religious Spirit," ask the Lord to give you a humble heart to see what you need to see and hear. Confess anything that comes to mind as you pray.
3. Ask the Holy Spirit to be your Teacher and to help you consider your life in light of His Word as you go through your study time.

Read

1. Read Chapter Thirteen, highlighting important parts that have particular meaning to your life.
2. Make notes of anything you need to apply to your life in the margins.
3. Also, jot down any areas that the Holy Spirit earmarks as needing prayer.

Apply

1. Look over anything you highlighted and reread these sections.
2. Using the notes you made in the margins, make any areas of application into goals by creating a list and a target date of completion.

Goal:

Goal:

Goal:

3. Answer the questions provided as a means of reviewing the material and creating the repetition necessary to have greater retention and understanding of these principles.

Fill in the blanks:

1. Loving God is the greatest _____ and the greatest ___ that we can receive. The second greatest commandment is to _____ our _____. If we keep these two commandments, we will _____ the _____ _____. Keeping these two _____ commandments to _____ will enable us to _____ all of the _____ "do nots" of the law.

2. Because loving God is our ___ _____, it must be the primary ___ of our ___. To divert us from this ultimate quest, the enemy uses one of his most ___ and ___ attacks upon the Church through the ___ _____. The devil wants to keep us focused on ___ in our _____ knowing that we will ___ what we are _____.

3. We should not ignore the _____ and ___ that are in our lives. The Scriptures command us to _____ ourselves and ___ ourselves to be sure that we are still in the _____. After iniquity is discovered, we should not turn to the Tree of ___ _____ ___ ___ ___ _____; we should turn to the Tree of _____. We should turn to the _____ of Jesus to find both _____ and _____ to overcome the sin.

4. The enemy tries to keep us away from the ___ of the Lord and the ___. This tactic comes in the form of a ___ _____, an evil spirit that is the _____ of the true ___ of God and true ___. This guise has probably done far more _____ to the Church than the New Age movement and all other cults _____.

5. A religious spirit is a _____ that seeks to substitute ___ _____ for the ___ of the ___ ___ in our lives. Its primary objective is to have the Church "holding to a _____ of _____, although they have _____ its _____...." The religious spirit does not ___ to the ___ or the _____ of the Church, it merely feeds the very ___ of man.

Matching:

6. a. Satan seems to understand even better than the Church that _____

   b. Satan's strategy is to _____

   c. If we do the will of God in pride _____

   d. Pride, by its very nature, _____

   1) make us proud, even proud of spiritual disciplines.

   2) our work will be counterproductive and could ultimately work toward our fall.

   3) is the most difficult stronghold to remove or correct.

   4) God resists the proud, but gives grace to the humble.

7. a. A religious spirit keeps us from hearing the voice of God by _____

   b. A religious spirit encourages _____

   c. We must get free of the religious spirit's deception _____

   d. The degree to which we have been delivered from religious spirit _____

   1) encouraging us to assume that we already know God's opinion.

   2) is the degree to which we can preach the true Gospel in power.

   3) the rationalization of Scripture so that correction is for everyone but us.

   4) so that we can worship the Lord in Spirit and truth.

8. a. We will never have the authority to deliver others _____

   b. To begin taking ground from the religious spirit, _____

   c. Jesus confronted the Pharisees continually _____

   d. We cannot focus on what is wrong with others _____

   1) while being blind to our own faults.

   2) about the religious spirit they had.

   3) until we are free ourselves.

   4) we must ask the Lord to shine His light on us first.

9. a. One of the most deceptive characteristics of the religious spirit _____
    b. Zeal for God is _____

    c. The enemy's strategy against zealous people _____
    d. The zealous people of Jesus' day _____

    1) crucified the Word Himself when He was among them.
    2) is that it is founded upon zeal for God.
    3) is to push them to glory in their own zeal.
    4) one of the most desperately needed characteristics of the Church today.

10. a. The religious spirit has done more damage to the Church _____
    b. The religious spirit has thwarted or diverted _____

    c. A manifestation of a religious spirit will _____
    d. The temple of God is no longer a building so the man of sin _____

    1) than all cults and more religions combined.
    2) take its seat in the very temple of God, claiming to be God.
    3) possibly every revival or movement to date.
    4) will take his seat in the Church.

Multiple Choice (there may be more than one true statement):

11. The religious spirit builds its work:
    a. on the motivation to please man
    b. on fear and pride
    c. to have us serve God to gain His approval
    d. to have us receive approval through the cross of Jesus
    e. on personal discipline rather than on the propitiatory sacrifice of Christ
12. Our deliverance from fear and pride:
    a. is usually a long process
    b. depends upon making amends for everything we have done through them
    c. means we must take up spiritual disciplines to counteract them
    d. depends on tearing up the roots through repentance and deliverance
13. People who have religious spirits:
    a. need our sharp rebuke

  b. need our patience

  c. need to be quickly removed from ministry until they are delivered

  d. must be thrown out of the Church

14. Guilt:

  a. can spur us on to great zeal for the Lord

  b. can make us offer sacrifices and offerings to atone for our failures

  c. -induced zeal is an affront to the cross

  d. is the wrong motive for pleasing God

  e. none of the above

15. Those gripped by a religious spirit:

  a. may be the ones most zealous to preach the cross

  b. emphasize their cross rather than the cross of Jesus

  c. delight in self-abasement

  d. are self-centered rather than God-centered

  e. none of the above

True or False:

16. Idealism is one of the most deceptive and destructive disguises of the religious spirit.

17. Idealism is possibly the most deadly enemy of true revelation and true grace.

18. Idealism will never condemn those who are not participating in the spiritual disciplines in the way they think best.

19. Idealism accepts the local church with its faults.

20. Perfectionism is a religious spirit founded upon pride.

21. Perfectionism points out inaccuracy but rarely points to solutions.

22. The religious spirit encourages the progress made along the path to growth.

23. The religious spirit knows that we are not complete in our understanding and therefore not 100 percent accurate.

24. The Lord's leadership style was to provide places where followers could make mistakes and learn from them.

25. A religious spirit built on both fear and pride can take self-abasement for failures to extremes.

26. A religious spirit built on both fear and pride will never feel superior to other Christians, making one unteachable.
27. A religious spirit built on both fear and pride will face confrontation with integrity.
28. A religious spirit will usually give a counterfeit gift of discernment, motivated by suspicion and fear.
29. A religious spirit's wisdom is rooted in the Tree of the Knowledge of Good and Evil, and though the truth may be accurate, it is ministered in a spirit that kills.
30. Suspicion is discernment motivated by love.
31. Any motivation other than love will distort spiritual perception.

Yield

1. Take the goals you have listed in the Apply section and pray over them. Ask the Holy Spirit to strengthen you to the task ahead as you grow in His likeness through these goals.
2. Devote prayer time to any areas the Holy Spirit earmarked as needing prayer. Look up Scriptures that speak to these areas and pray them over your life. Ask someone close to you to pray with you in any area that seems overwhelming to you.

Chapter Fourteen

ANGELS OF LIGHT

P-R-A-Y

Prepare

1. Get into a framework of spiritual warfare by finding a quiet place to focus your heart with thanksgiving, praise, and worship.
2. Using the title "Angels of Light," ask the Lord to give you a humble heart to see what you need to see and hear. Confess anything that comes to mind as you pray.
3. Ask the Holy Spirit to be your Teacher and to help you consider your life in light of His Word as you go through your study time.

Read

1. Read Chapter Fourteen, highlighting important parts that have particular meaning to your life.
2. Make notes of anything you need to apply to your life in the margins.
3. Also, jot down any areas that the Holy Spirit earmarks as needing prayer.

Apply

1. Look over anything you highlighted and reread these sections.
2. Using the notes you made in the margins, make any areas of application into goals by creating a list and a target date of completion.

Goal:

Goal:

Goal:

3. Answer the questions provided as a means of reviewing the material and creating the repetition necessary to have greater retention and understanding of these principles.

Answer the following:

1. What was Paul's warning to the Corinthians about those who ministered in a religious spirit? _____

2. To what specific heresy was Paul referring in Second Corinthians 11:13-15? _____

3. To what extent did this heresy go? What did Paul and the other apostles warn about this heresy? _____

4. What is a false apostle? What is an angel of light? _____

   _____

5. How do Messianic groups follow this heresy today? How do they thwart the spirit of Paul's writings? _____

   _____

6. How do adherents of this heresy display the empowerment of a religious spirit? _____

7. How does criticism appear to be wisdom? What does it actually come from? _____

True or False:

8. Believers who recognize the true grace of God look for ways to put others down.

9. Believers who are operating under God's grace find ways to build others up.

10. When Adam and Eve chose to live by the Knowledge of Good and Evil, they were partaking of the religious spirit.

11. The first result of Adam and Eve partaking of the religious spirit was becoming Christlike.

12. Cain is the first biblical model of a man controlled by the religious spirit.

13. The religious spirit will always try to keep us focused on the heavenly realm rather than the earthly realm.

14. The religious spirit judges by what is unseen rather than what is seen.

15. The fruit of labors will always be an acceptable offering to the Lord.

16. God will only accept the blood of the Lamb as an offering.

17. Those who attempt to live by their own works will often become enraged at those who take their stand on the righteousness of the Lamb.

18. Religions that are based on grace will easily become violent.

19. Those who are driven by religious spirits may well try to destroy people by means other than the physical taking of their lives.

20. The religious spirit rages against churches and ministries with onslaughts of slander.

Fill in the blanks:

21. In Ezekiel ___, the prophet was taken to a valley of ____ ____ and asked if the ____ ____ could ____. The Lord than commanded him to "____ **to the bones.**" As he ____, they came ____, came to ____, and then became a great ____.

22. The ____ prophet can see a great ___ in even the driest of ____. He will prophesy ____ to those bones until they come to ___ and then become an ___. A ____prophet with a religious spirit will do little more than just ___ the bones how ____ they are, heaping ____ and ____ on them, while imparting ___ ___ or ___ to overcome their ____.

23. Apostles and prophets are given ___ to ____ ____ and ____ ____, but we have no right to ____ ___ if we have not first ____ ____. We should give no one the ____ to bring ____ to the people under our care unless they first have a history of providing ____ ____ and ___ people up.

24. Prophets who do not have a ___ to build people ____ should be
_____ from _____. Jude said they are ____, ____ _____ who are
"hidden ___ in your love feasts."
25. Woe to the shepherds who ____ and____ for the sheep but fail to
____ them. Such is ____ tragic example.
26. The true grace of God is found between the ____ of _____ _____
and ____ ____ (approving of things that God ____). Either extreme
can be the result of a ___ ____.

Yield

1. Take the goals you have listed in the Apply section and pray over
them. Ask the Holy Spirit to strengthen you to the task ahead as you
grow in His likeness through these goals.
2. Devote prayer time to any areas the Holy Spirit earmarked as needing prayer. Look up Scriptures that speak to these areas and pray
them over your life. Ask someone close to you to pray with you in
any area that seems overwhelming to you.

Chapter Fifteen

OTHER MASKS OF
THE RELIGIOUS SPIRIT

Prepare

1. Get into a framework of spiritual warfare by finding a quiet place to focus your heart with thanksgiving, praise, and worship.
2. Using the title "Other Masks of the Religious Spirit," ask the Lord to give you a humble heart to see what you need to see and hear. Confess anything that comes to mind as you pray.
3. Ask the Holy Spirit to be your Teacher and to help you consider your life in light of His Word as you go through your study time.

Read

1. Read Chapter Fifteen, highlighting important parts that have particular meaning to your life.
2. Make notes of anything you need to apply to your life in the margins.
3. Also, jot down any areas that the Holy Spirit earmarks as needing prayer.

Apply

1. Look over anything you highlighted and reread these sections.
2. Using the notes you made in the margins, make any areas of application into goals by creating a list and a target date of completion.

Goal:

Goal:

Goal:

3. Answer the questions provided as a means of reviewing the material and creating the repetition necessary to have greater retention and understanding of these principles.

Multiple Choice (there may be more than one correct answer):

1. What is popularly called the "Jezebel spirit" is:
   a. a form of personality disorder
   b. a regularly displayed feminine mystique
   c. a form of the religious spirit
   d. an evil presumption on women in leadership

2. The Jezebel spirit:
   a. will be ambitious and manipulative
   b. will confound the wise and noble
   c. will make a claim for freedom
   d. will be found supplanting weak leadership

3. The Jezebel spirit:
   a. often makes a play for unusual action
   b. often uses a deceptively humble and submissive demeanor to manipulate
   c. usually gains its dominion by making political alliances
   d. is uncontrollable

4. Once this spirit gains authority:
   a. it weakens quickly
   b. it will usually manifest a strong control spirit
   c. it will deposit great frustration in a person's mind
   d. it will usually manifest shameless presumption

5. A telltale sign of prophets operating in a religious spirit is:
   a. that they are preoccupied with their own recognition
   b. that they are self-seeking
   c. that they speak truths from God
   d. that they are gifted oracles

6. The key difference between the false prophet and the true prophet is:
   a. that they like different kinds of churches in which to minister
   b. that their motivation is different
   c. that both desire to love the Lord
   d. that both desire to be recognized
7. The Jezebel spirit is:
   a. one of the greatest spiritual gifts to the Body of Christ
   b. one of the most beneficial ways to seek out the lost
   c. one of the most potent forms of the religious spirit
   d. seeking to keep the Church and the world from being prepared for the return of the Lord
   e. especially prone to attack the prophetic ministry because of its place in preparing the way of the Lord
   f. desirous of removing true prophets so that her false prophets can lead people intro idolatry and spiritual adultery
8. When there is a void of hearing the true voice of the Lord:
   a. people will be much more susceptible to deception
   b. religious leaders will be blind guides
   c. people will not recognize the Lord even when He speaks to them
   d. no one can do anything but wait
9. A primary strategy of a religious spirit is:
   a. to make us think that God is always good
   b. to push us into preaching the good news
   c. to get the Church to "sacrifice" in a way that perverts the command for us to take up our crosses daily
   d. to have us put more faith in our sacrifices than the Lord's sacrifice
   e. to use offerings and sacrifices to pressure God to manifest Himself
   f. to delude us into thinking that we can somehow purchase the grace and presence of God with our good works
   g. to acclaim the name of Jesus in new and fresh ways

True or False:

10. Conjuring is crucifying ourselves for the sake of righteousness, purification, spiritual maturity, or to get the Lord to manifest Himself.
11. Crucifying ourselves results in self-righteousness.
12. The pride of self-righteousness is not deceptive but bold and clear.
13. Crucifying ourselves gives the appearance of wisdom and righteousness.
14. The religious spirit makes us feel good about our wasted condition and deplorable sinful nature.
15. Pride never feels good; it feels debilitating.
16. Pride keeps our attention on how well we are doing and on how we stand compared to others—not on the glory of God.
17. We are not to neglect the disciplines, but when we take a perverse delight in doing them, rather than delighting in the Son of God, it is a religious spirit motivating us.

Matching:

18. a. Colossians 2:18-19 indicates that a person with a religious spirit _____
    b. A religious spirit wants to worship _____
    c. The same spirit that is given to worshiping angels _____

    d. Those with religious spirits will take _____

1) tends to delight in self-abasement.
2) anything or anyone but Jesus.
3) will also be prone to excessively exalting people.
4) improper stands on visions they have seen.

19. a. The fruit of true revelation will be _____
    b. In the last days there will be _____

    c. The danger is not from those who are having prophetic revelations but _____
    d. A religious spirit will always feed our _____

1) fear or pride.
2) an increase of prophecy, both true and false.
3) humility, not pride.
4) from those who have been inflated by them.

20. a. Genuine spiritual maturity ____

   b. Just like Paul, young apostles ____

   c. We need to hopefully be ____

   d. We should not be heading toward ____

   1) growing in grace and, therefore, humility.

   2) will always lead to increasing humility.

   3) being puffed up by our revelations or our accomplishments.

   4) can exude a lot of pride, but still be true apostles.

Fill in the blanks:

21. When combined with the religious spirit, the ___ ____ is one of the ___ and most ___ ____. To be a ___ martyr for the ___ and literally ___ our ___ for the sake of ___ is one of the greatest honors. Yet, when perverted, it is a most ___ form of _____.

22. When a religious spirit is combined with the ___ ____ it is almost ____ for that person to be ___ from the ____ that he is "suffering for the ___." Any rejection or ____ received from others is perceived as the ____ he must ____ to "___ for the ___." This ___ perspective drives him further from the ___ and any possibility of ___.

23. The martyr spirit can also be a manifestation of the spirit of ____. Those who have a _____ understanding of the cross ___ more in___ than they do in ___. They fail to see that the ___ of the cross is the ___, not the ___.

24. "Self-help psychology" attempts to _____ the power of the ___. It is humanistic-based psychology that Paul calls "a ___ ____." It is an ___ of the cross, and is another form of the ____ ____.

25. We all need "inner ___" to some degree, but much of what is being called ____ ____ is nothing more than digging up the "___ ____" and trying to get him ____. The answer to these deep wounds is not a ____ or ____, but simple ____. When we go to the ___ and find ____ and true ____ based on the ___ of Jesus, we will find a ___ ___ able to cast out all our ___ and ___ away all ___ and ____.

26. Deliverance is ____. Yet one of the enemy's major ___ is ____ the power of the _____ by having us _____ to it. We think it is not

acceptable unless it somehow seems ____ or ____. That is why we must become like ___ to enter the ____.

27. Adding to God's _____ is just as destructive as ___ ____ from them. If satan can get us to either ___ or ___ from the Word, then he knows our ___ is imminent, just as it was for Eve.

28. There are many "Christian" philosophies and _____ that ____ wise. Most are in fact attempting to be ___ for the ___ ___ in our lives. Some people do need counseling, and there are outstanding counselors who lead people to the ____. Others lead people into a ___ ____ of ____ that will ____ them and try to ___ in everyone else around them. This philosophy is an ___ of the cross of Christ.

Yield

1. Take the goals you have listed in the Apply section and pray over them. Ask the Holy Spirit to strengthen you to the task ahead as you grow in His likeness through these goals.

2. Devote prayer time to any areas the Holy Spirit earmarked as needing prayer. Look up Scriptures that speak to these areas and pray them over your life. Ask someone close to you to pray with you in any area that seems overwhelming to you.

Chapter Sixteen

THE WARNING SIGNS
OF A RELIGIOUS SPIRIT

Prepare

1. Get into a framework of spiritual warfare by finding a quiet place to focus your heart with thanksgiving, praise, and worship.
2. Using the title "The Warning Signs of a Religious Spirit," ask the Lord to give you a humble heart to see what you need to see and hear. Confess anything that comes to mind as you pray.
3. Ask the Holy Spirit to be your Teacher and to help you consider your life in light of His Word as you go through your study time.

Read

1. Read Chapter Sixteen, highlighting important parts that have particular meaning to your life.
2. Make notes of anything you need to apply to your life in the margins.
3. Also, jot down any areas that the Holy Spirit earmarks as needing prayer.

Apply

1. Look over anything you highlighted and reread these sections.
2. Using the notes you made in the margins, make any areas of application into goals by creating a list and a target date of completion.

Goal:

Goal:

Goal:

   3. Answer the questions provided as a means of reviewing the material and creating the repetition necessary to have greater retention and understanding of these principles.

Fill in the blanks:

   1. Almost ___ is battling the ____ ____ at least to some degree, and everyone's ___ is somewhat different. One may be dealing with ____ the issues to a small degree, and yet be more ___ from the ___ of the religious spirit than one who has _____ problems with just a couple of them.

   2. Our goal is to be ___ ___ of any ____ from the religious spirit by being ___ ____ to the ___ ____. Without complete ___ to the ____ there is ___ ___to be ___ from the religious spirit.

Fill in the chart:

   3. Add details about the warning signs of the religious spirit.

Warning Sign	Scripture Reference (from the text OR ones that come to mind)	Personal Notes
1. See their primary mission as the tearing down of whatever they believe is wrong		Where do I cause division and destruction?
2.		
3.		
4.		

5.		
6.		
7.		
8.		
9.		
10.		
11.		
12.		
13.		
14.		
15.		
16.		
17.		
18.		
19.		
20.		
21.		
22.		
23.		
24.		
25.		

Fill in the blanks:

4. When you read a list like the one above, if you continually think of how it relates to ___ ___, but really cannot see how much it ____ to ____, you may have the ____ ____ of all.

5. Those with a religious spirit usually have such a "____ in their own ___" that they cannot ____ their own ____.

6. Paul exhorted us: "____ ____ **to see if you are in the ___.**" He did not say to first test your ____, or test your ____, but to test ____. Using this text to ____ ____ can be a ____ that we have a ____ ____.

7. If the list above has given you ____ about problems in another ____, ____, or ____, be sure that you respond in the ____ ____, heeding Paul's warning to the Galatians: **"Brethren, if anyone is ___ in any ____, you who are ____, ____ such a one in the spirit of ____; each one looking to ____, lest you too be ____."**

8. It is the tendency of a religious spirit to ____ us from other ____. The tendency to cut off ____ with anyone because they have these ____ is an ____ that we have a ____ ____.

9. The Holy Spirit is called "___ ____" because that is His ____. If we are ____ the Holy Spirit, ____ will always be our tendency when someone else has ____. ____ helps.

Yield

1. Take the goals you have listed in the Apply section and pray over them. Ask the Holy Spirit to strengthen you to the task ahead as you grow in His likeness through these goals.

2. Devote prayer time to any areas the Holy Spirit earmarked as needing prayer. Look up Scriptures that speak to these areas and pray them over your life. Ask someone close to you to pray with you in any area that seems overwhelming to you.

Chapter Seventeen

Ten Things We Can Do to Get Free of the Religious Spirit

Prepare

1. Get into a framework of spiritual warfare by finding a quiet place to focus your heart with thanksgiving, praise, and worship.
2. Using the title "Ten Things We Can Do to Get Free of the Religious Spirit," ask the Lord to give you a humble heart to see what you need to see and hear. Confess anything that comes to mind as you pray.
3. Ask the Holy Spirit to be your Teacher and to help you consider your life in light of His Word as you go through your study time.

Read

1. Read Chapter Seventeen, highlighting important parts that have particular meaning to your life.
2. Make notes of anything you need to apply to your life in the margins.
3. Also, jot down any areas that the Holy Spirit earmarks as needing prayer.

Apply

1. Look over anything you highlighted and reread these sections.
2. Using the notes you made in the margins, make any areas of application into goals by creating a list and a target date of completion.

Goal:

Goal:

Goal:

3. Answer the questions provided as a means of reviewing the material and creating the repetition necessary to have greater retention and understanding of these principles.

Answer the following:

1. Why can a list of things we can do to get free of the religious spirit actually contribute toward being bound by one?

   _____

2. What is needed to keep us from taking a "how-to" list for getting rid of the religious spirit and creating more religious activity?

   _____

3. Fill in the chart below:

Guidelines to Draw Close to God	Scripture Reference (from the text OR ones that come to mind)	Personal Notes
1. Develop a secret relationship with the Lord.	John 5:44	Where do I want others to notice my spiritual disciplines or religious activity? Where do I seek glory from people rather than the glory of my God?

2.		
3.		
4.		
5.		
6.		
7.		
8.		
9.		
10.		

Fill in the blanks:

4. Basically, the religious spirit seeks to _____ the Holy Spirit as the ___ of ___ ____. It does this by seeking to replace ___ ____, which leads to ____, with a repentance based on our ____. The effect is to replace true ____ with ____.

5. True religion is based on ___ the Lord and then ___ our _____. True religion will promote ___ and ____ founded on ___ for the Lord rather than the ___ or ____ for ____ or ____.

6. The religious spirit is basically a ____ of the "good" side of the ___ of the ___ of ___ and ____. When Adam and Eve ate of that tree in the Garden, the first result was that they _____ at _____. Self-centeredness is the ____ that made that fruit ____, and it is still the most ____ ____ the serpent seeks to give us.

7. The Holy Spirit will always lead us into a life that is ____-_____. This is in contrast to the religious spirit which causes us to focus our attention on ____ and base our concept of the Christian life on

    ____.

8. The Holy Spirit produces fruit by ___ us to the Lord and applying the ___ He accomplished for us on the ____. We must understand

that this is the cross of ____ and not our ____ cross. We are called to deny ___ and take up our ___ ___, but we are not to ___ in ___-____ or try to live by the ___ of our own ____. Rather, we are to glory in what Jesus ____and the sacrifice that ___ made.

True or False:

9. We have our standing before God solely on the basis of the crosses we bear daily.
10. Our ability to come before the throne of God has everything to do with whether we have had a good or bad day.
11. Our acceptance before God is based on the sacrifice Jesus made for our justification.
12. Christ's sacrifice negates our need for personal holiness.
13. If we are joined to Christ, we can still go on living in sin.
14. We do not become free from sin in order to abide in Christ, but by abiding in Him we become free from sin.
15. If Jesus is not our Life, then we do not really know the Way or the Truth either.
16. It is the religious spirit that tries to keep Christianity in the realm of the Way and the Truth, while keeping us from the essential union by which Jesus becomes our Life.
17. True Christianity involves not just what we believe, but who we believe.
18. True worship has its purpose in seeing the Lord.
19. When we see the Lord, we will worship.
20. When we see the glory of the Lord, we become captivated by our own positive or negative qualities, instead of His beauty.

Answer the following:

21. What is the goal of true faith? How does the Book of Revelation demonstrate this? _____

_____

22. Contrast the way in which the world is increasingly repulsed by religion with how Jesus will draw people unto Him. _____

_____

_____

23. What happens when we are truly joined to Jesus? _____
    _____

Yield

1. Take the goals you have listed in the Apply section and pray over them. Ask the Holy Spirit to strengthen you to the task ahead as you grow in His likeness through these goals.
2. Devote prayer time to any areas the Holy Spirit earmarked as needing prayer. Look up Scriptures that speak to these areas and pray them over your life. Ask someone close to you to pray with you in any area that seems overwhelming to you.

ANSWER KEY

Introduction: Satan's Cord of Three Strands

1. Personal answer of the reader
2. Personal answer based on the reader's experience and the fact that multiple forces or three "strands of a cord" are more difficult to break than just one cord or one force.
3. Truth, because truth breaks the power of evil
4. Personal answer of the reader based on the Scripture
5. return, occupied, return, seven, evil spirits, powerful
6. evil, fill, truth, Holy Spirit
7. deception, truth, counterpower
8. righteousness, truth, evil
9. tests, much fruit, free, free, strongholds
10. together, interrelationships, strategies, together
11. a-3, b-5, c-1, d-2, e-4
12. false
13. true
14. true
15. false
16. true
17. e
18. Personal name inserted into Scripture

Chapter One: The Ultimate Powers of Evil

1. Racism is rooted in two yokes that hold people in bondage (fear and pride); it binds humankind and is the primary stronghold that empowers the spirit of death; many people believe they are free from prejudice, but they are deceived.
2. Fear and pride; racism is due to either pride in the flesh or fear of those who are different, creating a thick veil over the human soul.
3. The nations that will rise against each other and the kingdoms that will clash will do so because of ethnic conflict; "nation" is the Greek word

ethnos and describes how ethnic differences will be one of the greatest issues facing the world and the Church in the last days.

4. Because racism's cause is a spiritual power, only that which is bound in Heaven can be bound on earth; the Church must overcome racism within its own ranks so that we can take spiritual authority over it.

5. The world will fall into an abyss of chaos, destruction, and suffering of unprecedented proportions; "dismay among nations [ethnos] in perplexity" at the things to come, including fear and shaking.

6. Personal response from reader including current or recent political wars and conflicts

7. true
8. true
9. false
10. true
11. false
12. false
13. true
14. true
15. two; pride; externals; sufficient; fear; fall; insecure; different; control
16. relationships; trust; establishes; forgiveness; trust; possible; fear; pride; division
17. cross; overcomes; man; insecurity; cross; grace; forgiveness; pride; dependency; trust
18. works; humble; secure; tolerance; different; spiritual; flesh
19. flesh; Christ; no longer; Christ; new creature; passed away; new
20. rest; wisdom; understanding; counsel; strength; knowledge; fear; delight; fear; judge; eyes see; decision; ears hear
21. b, c
22. d
23. a, b, c
24. a, d
25. b, d
26. d
27. b

Chapter: Two The Tyranny of the Familiar

1. It keeps them from breaking out of their sociological and economic barriers.
2. We are afraid of change, and we tend to put our security in our environment instead of in the Lord.
3. A strong trust must be built as a bridge out of our situation.
4. They are not willing to sacrifice the time and effort necessary.
5. a-3; b-1; c-2; d-5; e-4

6. d
7. a
8. c
9. a, b, c, d
10. a, b, c
11. true
12. true
13. false
14. false
15. true
16. true
17. stripes; healed; authority; wounded
18. cross; healing; wounds; loving; power; free; love
19. prophetic; Christ; free; freedom; salvation
20. healed; revival; liberty; nation
21. inner sanctuary; glory; presence; move; America
22. d
23. c
24. sheep; goats; sheep; goats; sheep; sheep; goats
25. Personal answer based upon the principle that separation of sheep and goats is because of acceptance issues, being kind to all people.
26. Personal answer based upon the idea that, as America was founded upon embracing all people, no matter what class, race, gender, or culture, God has poured out blessings to create our status as a world power.
27. Personal answer based upon the concept that fear and pride cause racism. Humility, therefore, opens us up to the grace of God (see James 4:6), and thereby we build each other up rather than tearing each other down.

Chapter Three: Healing Cultural Wounds

1. b, c
2. b, d
3. a, c
4. d
5. d
6. b, d
7. true
8. false
9. false
10. false
11. false
12. true
13. elders; hospitable; aliens; foreigners
14. open; different; leadership

15. value; proud; insecure; leadership
16. a-4; b-3; c-2; d-1
17. a-2; b-1; c-4; d-3
18. Yes; there will be conflict in the future because there are procedures and doctrines that will create disagreement.
19. Church unity will come by a commitment to truth. No, we do not need to compromise our convictions. Many of those who oppose us may help bring balance to the Body of Christ.
20. Most church splits are not caused by doctrine or procedure but by territorial preservation, which is a deadly and selfish evil.
21. It has killed churches and movements because we put up dividing walls that break our true unity under the cross.
22. This barrier is related to racism as it tries to blur the distinctions between men and women so that the husband and wife are not two becoming one flesh. Husbands and wives must learn to relate in their own distinct roles.
23. Because the other gender's perception helps give information that we cannot see on our own about the world and the Lord.
24. We need to recognize that we need each other and respect our differences. We need men and women to learn how to relate to each other properly. The cross is the ultimate place of healing for men and women.
25. The priest carried the stones of all the tribes of Israel on his chest = we must carry all of God's people on our hearts.
26. The Church must see others with the Lord's eyes, hear people with the Lord's ears, love people with the Lord's heart—spiritual fruit from our abiding will affect the world.
27. Jesus did not judge by His natural eyes or ears; He judged by what the Father revealed—this contrasts how we often expect to receive discernment from the media or what we see with our own eyes, which doesn't reveal the true story behind the story that only God knows.

Chapter Four: A Practical Strategy

1. true
2. true
3. false
4. false
5. true
6. a-2; b-4; c-1; d-3
7. a-3; b-1; c-4; d-2
8. 2000; 2000; Jew; Gentile; creation; Christ
9. diversity; conformity; joined; spiritual; new creation
10. purpose; arrogant; branches; fear; spare; natural; spare you
11. natural; impugn; integrity; Abraham; Old Testament
12. humility; see; purpose; natural; humility; natural; purpose; Church

13. c
14. d
15. b
16. It distorts reality by only reporting the most extreme events, which are often acts of violence.
17. Personal answer regarding how what media thinks is newsworthy is not reflective of the majority of Americans.
18. The Christian media does not report the day-to-day ministries of average churches because it is not spectacular enough to be "news."
19. They focus on actions or statements that are either cute, funny, or dramatic because otherwise they would be boring.
20. They blur reality and reduce our perceptions; they subtly train us to respond only to extremes.
21. d
22. a
23. c
24. a
25. b
26. a, d
27. a, b, c, d, e
28. b, c

Chapter Five: The Two Ministries

1. continually; intercession; accusation; battle; Kingdom; God; kingdom; darkness
2. Church; dwelling; throne; heart; Church
3. intercessor; priest; abide; use; intercede; house; prayer; all; nations
4. accuser; brethren; accuses; day; night; access; lives; accuse; criticize
5. saints; access; accusing; brethren
6. a, c
7. b
8. a, c
9. a, b, c, d
10. b, d
11. c, d, e, f
12. Because whenever we criticize someone else, we assume we are superior to them.
13. Something that we should fear the most—God's resistance (James 4:6)
14. The Fall, Peter's betrayal of the Lord, and other examples
15. We are not good in and of ourselves. When we condemn others, we put ourselves in jeopardy of falling to the same sins.
16. a-4, b-2, c-1, d-3

17. a-2, b-4, c-1; d-3
18. c
19. a
20. The critical person is critical of everyone but himself; the accepting person is critical of himself first. The critical person cannot see his own problems; the accepting person is open to seeing his own faults. The critical person looks for specks in the eyes of others and cannot see the log in his own eye; the accepting person checks his judgments through the filter of his own faults and shortcomings.
21. He warns us that it would be better for us not to have been born (see Matt. 18).
22. First, go to the person. If he rejects your counsel, second, go to the person with another Christian. If he rejects the second counsel, third, go before the rest of the church with the issue.
23. Jesus said to us "Depart from Me, you who practice lawlessness" (Matt. 7:23). Unrighteous judgment will keep many from entering the Kingdom of Heaven.
24. We are to follow the procedure, even when we know someone will not listen to us. We are also to be sure that people in public ministry are not exempt from this procedure.
25. We are not to execute judgment but to intercede.
26. We are not to speak about the sin with anyone else or to make it public.
27. Examples of answers: We want someone else's "opinion." We feel that someone else should "pray" for that person. But it is still gossip.

Chapter: Six Love and Vision

1. First Peter 4:8—"Love covers a multitude of sins."
2. No, He usually deals with one or two at a time because we could not handle everything at the same time. It would result in frustration and defeat.
3. Matthew 18 was written for when there is injury beyond our personal offense. We are not to beat each other up or even inform our brother of our offense. Our love should cover most of these sins. We must not use this out of self-preservation or retaliation.
4. He first praised the church and highlighted what they were doing right. He then straightforwardly addressed their problems. He gave them opportunity to repent. He then gave each church a wonderful promise of reward for overcoming their problems. We are to wrap our correction in encouragement, hope, and promises.
5. He accuses us through condemnation, imparting hopelessness. He tears us down, trying to get us to quit. His goal is always destruction.

6. Personal answers, which may include the following:

Scripture	Key Words/ Concepts	Instruction for Our Discernment
1 Cor. 5:12	Within the Church	Criticism can be rooted in true discernment
Prov. 6:12-15	Worthless person Perverse mouth, heart Points fingers Sows discord	Much "discernment" is actually suspicion to mask territorial preservation
James 3:13-18	Wise and under-standing=good conduct Bitterness and envy=lie against the truth Wisdom from earth or above	Earthly wisdom = sensual and demonic Wisdom from above = pure, peaceable, gentle, yielding, merciful, full of grace If we want grace and mercy we must show grace and mercy
Matt. 5:21-26	Anger can = mur-ders judgment Be reconciled then offer gift Agree with adversary quickly	Slander is cause for us to stop and reconcile before bringing our offering to God. We are locked in prisons made by our judgments Must pay the last cent
1 John 4:20	Christian who doesn't love others = a liar Seen Unseen	How we treat people is essential to our salvation How we treat people shows whether we love God or not
1 John 3:15-16	Hate = murder Love = laying down one's life	If we really have Christ's Spirit, we will also possess His nature Christ's love was not conditional, and ours should not be either Denial and desertion from friends is not just cause to criticize and not love them

7. true
8. true
9. false
10. true
11. false
12. false
13. false
14. true
15. false
16. false
17. true
18. leaders; opposers; persecutors
19. serving faithfully; vessels; accuser; stumbling block
20. never; leaders; guilty; pride
21. restoration; light; new; lost
22. jealousy; faithful; time; worthy; use; restoration; truth; purposes
23. humility; nature; prepared; joy; further
24. better; disqualify; further; commands; honor; natural; spiritual; longevity
25. sever; faith; humility; opportunity

Chapter Seven: The Heart of the Freedom Fighter

Answers for 1-8 will be personal to the reader but contain some of the following:

1. "Spiritual eunuchs." Just like an eunuch, whose joy was for the king's pleasure with the bride, so we must use our ministry, our reputation, and those who serve with us in order to please our King.
2. no selfishness; no empty conceit; humility of mind; regarding others as more important than self; look out for others' interests; equality is not to be grasped at; empty self; become obedient even to the point of death
3. Humility will be rewarded with exaltation; self-exaltation will be rewarded with humility; God raises us up; we don't.
4. In the presence of the Lord. In His presence we will always find purity, and we can hear and see with pure senses and therefore do the will of the Father.
5. Under the mighty hand of God. If we are under His hand, we will know that He is exalting us and not we ourselves.
6. Leaders begin to be afraid that someone might be better than they are and try to hang on to old wineskins; other leaders do not want to give away what they have worked for over a long period of time to someone who doesn't seem to have "paid the same price" as they have.
7. The older generation can put stumbling blocks in front of the newer generation in terms of traditional methods or withholding their sanction or blessings; the younger generation can presume that they know everything

and through arrogance put off the older ways as being incorrect when they are not. Both reveal spiritual pride.

8. John knew the boundaries of his ministry and recognized the gifts of Jesus. He honored Jesus in front of his "congregation" and disciples, pointing to Him as the way to go. Jesus recognized the ministry of John to His congregation and disciples, giving John credit for the way in which God used him. And Jesus had John baptize him to show the submission He had to God's plan for each one of them.

9. true
10. false
11. true
12. false
13. true
14. b, d
15. a, d
16. c
17. c
18. a
19. persecuted; persecute; pride; generations; concluded
20. grace; cross; heart; mistreat
21. hope; spiritual; further; rejoice
22. lives; next; smooth; possible; rejoice; decrease; arises
23. spirit; return; fathers; sons; sons; fathers
24. prepares; ultimate purposes; ministries; accusation; intercession
25. pointing; finger; criticisms; intercession
26. critical; light; healing' answered prayer; glory; revealed
27. intercession; restore; foundations; breach; humankind; people

Chapter Eight: Understanding Witchcraft

1. Christianity; attack; witchcraft; nature; overcome; crucial; all
2. ignorance; complacency; position; full armor; vigilant; stand; prevail
3. counterfeit spiritual; other; dominate; manipulate; control; carnal nature; demonic
4. pressure; manipulate; hype; power; service; God; scheme; pressure points; manipulative
5. walk; true authority; truth; trusting; Lord; concerns; keys; free; influence; pressure
6. true spiritual; manifested; Kingdom; authority; influence; trusted; establish; ordained
7. influence; manipulation; self-promotion; stumbling block; true authority; true; utterly trust; His time
8. true
9. false

10. true
11. false
12. false
13. true
14. true
15. a-4; b-1; c-2; d-3
16. a-2; b-4; c-3; d-1
17. a-4; b-3; c-1; d-2
18. a-4; b-1; c-2; d-3
19. c, d
20. a, b
21. b, c, d, e
22. a, d
23. b, c, d
24. White witchcraft in the Church can be described as "charismatic witch-craft." It is pseudo-spirituality that tries to gain influence or control of others or situations. It is the source of many false prophecies, dreams, and visions. These people think they know the mind of the Lord, which gives them greater authority.
25. Jezebel used her power to control her husband, Ahab, who was king. She caused the prophet Elijah to enter into a great depression. Jezebel represents what we face today when people are ignorant of the potential that witchcraft has.
26. Satan does not confront God's people with power. He distracts and seduces them with deception.
27. Our first defense is to maintain humility, knowing we are standing only by God's grace. This eliminates the breach in our armor that pride can cause.

Chapter Nine: The Stings of Witchcraft

1. In a series of stings; the successive stings target those areas of previous stings to build upon one another. The cumulative effect overwhelms us.
2. discouragement; confusion; depression; loss of vision; disorientation; withdrawal; despair; defeat; personal answer and definition by reader for each of the above
3. It can happen quickly, but more often it works slowly so that we don't see the attacks as being linked.
4. satanic cults, New Age operatives, well-meaning deceived Christians; Personal response to the rest of this question
5. They can pray against leaders rather than for them. Their misguided prayers have power because whatever is released on earth is released in Heaven. Intercession motivated by control or manipulation can be devastating.
6. misguided prayer, gossip, political maneuvering, jealousy
7. We can become resentful or bitter toward that person and fall into the progression of witchcraft's stings.

8. We must respond only by the Holy Spirit and bear His fruit (love, joy, peace, etc.). We must not respond in any other spirit or try to combat the enemy in our own strength. We must remember that satan cannot cast out satan so we cannot cast out Jezebel if we have a Jezebel spirit ourselves.
9. We need to bless those who curse us. We don't bless their works, but we pray for them and not against them. We do not retaliate and thereby receive the same spirit.
10. Our battle is not against flesh and blood; it is spiritual. The weapons of our warfare are not carnal but spiritual. Praying blessings on our attackers results in the evil power of control and manipulation being broken over their lives and our lives. We must overcome evil with good.

11.

Progression	Sting	Source Notes
1	Discouragement	No apparent reason Difficulties seem insurmountable Want to give up even though things haven't become worse
2	Confusion	No apparent reason Lose clarity about what we have been called to do Weakens resolve and compounds discouragement
3	Depression	Unshakeable dread Combination of discouragement and confusion + general negligence in spiritual disciplines
4	Loss of Vision	Doubt that God called us to the task in the first place Difficulty holding our course Drifting in circles
5	Disorientation	Forgotten our course and lost ability to read the compass Scriptures no longer speak to us Struggle to trust the Lord's voice or receive encouragement Spiritual incapacitation, inability to function

6	Withdrawal	Retreating from our purpose in the ministry Withdrawing from fellowship with the rest of the church Can also bring withdrawal from our families
7	Despair	Hopelessness that brings vulnerability Easy target for enemy through temptation, sickness, or death Deterioration of body
8	Defeat	Weakening to fall further and further behind Easy to get picked off

12. false
13. true
14. true
15. false
16. true
17. false
18. true
19. true
20. destroy, battle; finish
21. use; slave; guile; turn; tables
22. Ephesians; flesh; blood; principalities; powers
23. spiritual warfare; survive; fight

Chapter Ten: Victory Over Witchcraft

1. By the blood of the Lamb, the word of our testimony, and not loving our lives even unto death. We overcome as we take our stand on what Christ has already accomplished for us by the cross. The word of our testimony is the Scriptures, countering the enemy's temptation with God's truth, which is our only offensive weapon in the armor of God. Not loving our lives unto death means that we have the utter commitment to follow Him, regardless of the price.
2. Personal answer showing our vulnerability to attack when we are focused on self.
3. We see ourselves crucified with Christ and this means the enemy doesn't have access to us because he has no more access to Him. If we are dead to this world, nothing can defeat us.
4. Without all three, we can make occasional, halting advances, but we will sooner or later be pushed back.

5. Yes, scriptural prophecy confirms that the Lord, the Church, and the truth are going to prevail. Satan will be cast down to earth and bring a time of trouble unlike any other, but we will prevail.
6. We will marvel at the pitiful nature of the one who caused so much trouble.
7. The glory of the Lord will appear on His people much brighter because of the degree of darkness.
8. We must fight like we are going to win, giving no more ground to the enemy and taking back what he has usurped. We must resist satan until he flees from us. Then we must pursue him until he is driven out of others.
9. a-1; b-4; c-3; d-2
10.

Overcoming	Principles to Remember	Personal Notes
Discouragement	God does not author discouragement; He authors faith He is the source of hope, not disappointment His correction is peaceable and gentle	I need to reject discouragement quickly and instinctively I must not let discouragement dictate my course I must keep my my shield of faith up
Confusion	God does not author confusion Nothing goes as planned, so be ready for the confusion	Use any confusion to my advantage Anticipate confusion Look for an opportunity to gain an advantage over the enemy Resolve to stand and fight
Depression	Depression is usually the result of allowing discouragement and confusion to cause us to drift from spiritual disciplines	Continue practicing spiritual disciplines, like reading the Word, praying, fellowshiping, etc. even when I don't feel like it
Loss of Vision	Turn loss of vision against the enemy by recommitting to the vision more than ever before Establish my purpose on the Word Holding the curse is essential	I need to record visions and words that the Lord gives to me so I can read and reread them when I need to I need to search the Scriptures to establish myself more firmly in what He has done and what He will do

Overcoming Disorientation	We cannot trust our feelings We must rely on our spiritual "instruments"—the Word of God	I need to receive my guidance, not based on my current feelings, but on those things that ground me—the Word and its testimony
Overcoming Withdrawal	There are no "time-outs" in God We cannot let our guard down We are on the front line of spiritual battle each day Our times of relief are even to be guarded with vigilance Strategic retreats are different than withdrawing from battle Quitting is defeat Repentance is an adjustment that will result in further victories Repentance comes because of truth that sets us free Defeat will result in a spiritual bondage to the power of the enemy	If I over-commit myself, I need to hold my ground until my position can be strengthened Even if I have acted presumptuously, I must not quit but instead repent
Overcoming Despair	We are social creatures and need each other Withdrawing from fellowship helps us sink into the deepest pit of hopelessness Fellowship is the remedy	When I feel hopeless, I must return to fellowship to get help to reverse the slide
Overcoming Defeat	Defeat is temporary if we look to God, who will bring ultimate victory He will bring us to victory in everything that He has called us to do	I need to remember that attacks may defeat me, but I do not need to be destroyed I must remember that I can overwhelmingly conquer through Him who loves me

Chapter Eleven: Combating New Age Witchcraft

1. witchcraft; Hinduism; acceptable; white-collar; numerous; wealthiest; powerful; unsuccessful
2. valuable commodity; accumulating, interpreting; packaging; transferring; largest; knowledge; degree
3. fellowship; spiritual void; supernatural; neutrality; supernatural power; evil; counterfeit supernatural powers
4. words; power; words; doctrines; conquering; power; fundamental aspect
5. power; believing; hearts; minds; power; believing minds
6. gifts; Spirit; tests; separate; believers; creeds; doctrines; foolish; wise
7. a-2; b-4; c-1; d-3
8. b, c, e
9. c, d
10. a, c
11. d, e
12. No, being "open to the gifts" is usually a cop-out for those who are fearful of them. Earnestly desiring means to ask, seek, and knock.
13. No, this is not biblical. The two are not mutually exclusive. We are to seek the Giver more than the gifts, but we are commanded to seek the gifts as part of seeking God.
14. We were all created for fellowship in the Spirit, which is by definition supernatural. Although some Christians often claim that God no longer moves supernaturally, we cannot have fellowship with God unless we desire the supernatural because God is supernatural.
15. The true Word of God is verified by the true power of God. Jesus went about to **"do and teach"** (Acts 1:1). He usually performed miracles before He taught. He knew that an undeniable encounter with God would make people open to His words.
16. Because witchcraft is counterfeit spiritual authority, we will only be completely free from the power of witchcraft when we are completely submitted to the authority of God. If our spiritual void is not filled with the real power and authority of God, we will become subject to witchcraft in some form. We will either choose the power and authority of God or the power and authority of the evil one—but we will all choose.
17. a-3; b-1; c-4; d-2
18. a-4; b-3; c-2; d-1
19. a-2; b-4; c-1; d-3
20. a-2; b-3; c-1; d-4
21. true
22. true
23. false
24. false
25. false

26. true
27. true
28. false
29. true

Chapter Twelve: Witchcraft in the Media

1. d
2. b
3. a
4. c
5. c
6. c
7. true
8. false
9. true
10. false
11. false
12. true
13. true
14. elders; protection; direction; standards; influence; high standards
15. manipulate; policy; massive influence
16. standards; elders; ministries; standards; authority; stumbling blocks; procedures
17. wisdom; truth; Truth Himself; righteousness; holiness; truth; self; philosophy; world
18. b, c
19. a, b, c, d
20. e
21. a, c, d
22. b, c, e
23. b, d
24. c, d
25. a, b, c, d
26. b

Chapter Thirteen: Understanding the Religious Spirit

1. commandment; gift; love; neighbors; keep; whole law; positive; love; obey; negative
2. highest goal; focus; lives; deceptive; deadly; religious spirit; evil; lives; become; beholding
3. sins; errors; examine; test; faith; the Knowledge of Good and Evil; Life; cross; forgiveness; power

4. glory; cross; religious spirit; counterfeit; love; worship; damage; combined

5. demon; religious activity; power; Holy Spirit; form; godliness; denied; power; add; life; power; pride

6. a-4; b-1; c-2; d-3

7. a-1; b-3; c-4; d-2

8. a-3; b-4; c-2; d-1

9. a-2; b-4; c-3; d-1

10. a-1; b-3; c-2; d-4

11. b, c, e

12. a, d

13. b, c

14. a, b, c, d

15. a, b, c, d

16. true

17. true

18. false

19. false

20. true

21. true

22. false

23. false

24. true

25. true

26. false

27. false

28. true

29. true

30. false

31. true

Chapter Fourteen: Angels of Light

1. They were false apostles, deceitful workers; just as satan disguised himself as an angel of light, his servants disguised themselves as servants of righteousness

2. Jews were seeking to bring Gentile converts under the yoke of the Law of Moses.

3. Many different cities were deceived by this heresy. The apostles warned that, if believers turned back to the Law of Moses, it would actually sever them from Christ (see Gal. 5:4).

4. A false apostle is one who looks as if they have widespread spiritual authority over a region, but they fail to represent the Kingdom of God

in at least one or more major areas. An angel of light is someone who disguises themselves as a servant of righteousness, using truths for the purpose of destruction. Quoting Scripture and using wisdom is often part of this, but it comes from the Tree of Knowledge and it is wisdom that kills.

5. They base their identity on the flesh instead of the Spirit through being born again into Christ. They are not well-grounded in the New Covenant. These groups convince people that they are the lost tribes of Israel, undermining the pure message of the Gospel of grace, about which Paul so passionately wrote.

6. They have a tendency to focus on what is wrong with Christians or the Church, instead of on what is right. Although its guise is to protect the sheep or truth or the Lord's glory, the religious spirit is an evil, critical spirit that will always end up causing division and destruction.

7. Criticism can make us sound like we know what we are talking about and have an awareness of something that others do not have. But it is really pride in one of its basest forms. When we criticize, we are in effect declaring ourselves to be better than others. If we are better than someone else in any area, it is only by God's grace.

8. false
9. true
10. true
11. false
12. true
13. false
14. false
15. false
16. true
17. true
18. false
19. true
20. true
21. 37; dry bones; dry bones; live; prophesy; prophesied; together; life; army
22. true; army; bones; life; life; army; false; tell; dry; discouragement; condemnation; no life; power; circumstances
23. authority; build up; tear down; tear down; built up; authority; correction; spiritual nourishment; building
24. heart; up; eliminated; ministry; grumblers; fault finders; reefs
25. feed; care; correct; Eli's
26. extremes; unrighteous faultfinding; unsanctified mercy; condemns; religious spirit

Chapter Fifteen: Other Masks of the Religious Spirit

1. c
2. a, d
3. b, c
4. b, d
5. a, b
6. b
7. c, d, e f
8. a, b, c
9. c, d, e, f
10. true
11. true
12. false
13. true
14. false
15. false
16. true
17. true
18. a-1; b-2; c-3; d-4
19. a-3; b-2; c-4; d-1
20. a-2; b-4; c-1; d-3
21. martyr syndrome; ultimate; deadly delusions; true; faith; lose; lives; Christ; tragic; deception
22. martyr syndrome; impossible; delivered; deception; Gospel; correction; price; pay; stand; truth; warped; truth; correction
23. suicide; perverted; glory; death; life; point; resurrection; grave
24. replace; cross; different gospel; enemy; religious spirit
25. healing; inner healing; old man; healed; procedure; formula; forgiveness; cross; forgiveness; acceptance; blood; perfect love; fears; wash: bitterness; resentment
26. simple; strategies; diluting; Gospel; add; brilliant; abstract; children; Kingdom
27. commandments; taking away; add; subtract; fall
28. therapies; seem; substitutes; Holy Spirit; cross; black hole; self-centeredness; consume; suck; enemy

Chapter Sixteen: The Warning Signs of a Religious Spirit

1. everyone; religious spirit; fight; all; free; yoke; serious
2. completely free; influence; completely submitted; Holy Spirit; submission; Lord; no way; free

3.

Warning Sign	Scripture Reference (from the text OR ones that come to mind)	Personal Notes (these will be personal to the reader)
1. See their primary mission as the tearing down of whatever they believe is wrong		Where do I cause division and destruction?
2. Unable to accept a rebuke, especially from those they judge to be less spiritual		Where have I had a hard time accepting rebuke? What has been my response to someone who has corrected me?
3. Has a philosophy of listening only to God, not to people		Do I have spiritual pride that does not allow me to listen to others?
4. Inclined to see more of what is wrong than what is right (with others, churches, etc.)		Is my perspective distorted so that I tend to see only what people are doing and not what God is doing?
5. Subject to an overwhelming feeling of guilt that they can never measure up to the Lord's standards.		In what situations or patterned sin do I feel guilt? Where do I have trouble simply abiding in Christ?
6. Keep score on their spiritual life		Where do I feel better just because I did something like attend meetings or read my Bible, rather than because I got closer to God through the experience?
7. Believe that they have been appointed to fix everyone else		Where do I feel that I have appointed myself the sheriff or watchman of God's Kingdom? Where have I not helped to build my local church but have been more of an annoyance?
8. Have a leadership style that is bossy, overbearing, intolerant of the weakness or failure of others	James 3:17-18	Where do I find people cowering or thinking I am too bossy? Where do I have a hard time tolerating others?

9. Feel that they are closer to God than others, or their lives or ministries are more pleasing to Him		Have I been deluded into thinking that I am drawing closer to God because of who I am rather than through Jesus?
10. Take pride in their spiritual maturity and discipline, especially as compared to others		How do I compare myself to others? Have I lost sight of my true goal—Jesus?
11. Believe that they are on the "cutting edge" of what God is doing		Do I feel that what I am involved in is the most important thing God is doing right now?
12. Will have a mechanical prayer life		Do I feel relief when my prayer time is over? Do I truly treasure the time I have with God?
13. Will do things to be noticed by others		Am I guilty of idolatry because I fear what people think more than what God thinks?
14. Will be overly repulsed by emotionalism	2 Sam. 6:14-16	Where do I think there are excesses? When does my leadership say we are encountering the true life of God, but I find the experience carnal, too emotional, or excessive?
15. Use emotionalism as a substitute for the work of the Holy Spirit		Have I been driven to self-preservation and exaltation through the use of weeping and wailing during times of repentance, or falling under the power easily? Do I see these as requirements or as possible expressions as the Holy Spirit directs?
16. Are encouraged when their ministries look better than others		Am I anxious to be better than someone else? Does it bother me when someone else's ministry looks better than mine?
17. Glory more in what God did in the past		Do I forget that God has not changed? Do I make

than what He is doing in the present		comparisons with past works rather than simply draw closer to the Lord?
18. Tend to be suspicious of, or opposed to, new movements, churches, etc.		Do I find myself thinking that if God is not doing a new thing in me, He can't be doing it with anyone else?
19. Tend to reject spiritual manifestations that they do not understand	1 Thess. 5:21	Do I presume that my opinion is the same as God's? Am I teachable, humble, open, patient, watchful for fruit before I make judgments?
20. Overreact to carnality in the Church		Do I take any discernment that I have and distort it to rarely see growth in people, even if it seems slow?
21. Overreact to immaturity in the Church		Do I only see immaturity, without considering the other factors that contribute to someone's spiritual age?
22. Overly prone to view supernatural manifestations as evidence of God's approval		Do I keep score, comparing myself with others as to what miracles they have received versus what I have received? Do I build my reputation on these miracles?
23. Unable to join anything that they do not deem perfect or nearly perfect		Do I forget that the Lord joined the imperfect human race, of which I am a part? Do I abide in Him and give my life as He did, regardless of the imperfections of others?
24. Overly paranoid of the religious spirit		Do I fear the religious spirit or do I exercise my faith to overcome it in Jesus?
25. Tend to glory in anything but the cross of Jesus, what He has accomplished, and who He is		How shaky is my foundation? Do I see the pillar of my ministry and life as the Lord, or have I replaced Him in any areas?

4. someone else; applies; you; biggest problem
5. log; eye; see; problems
6. Test yourselves; faith; neighbor; pastor; yourselves; measure others; symptom; serious problem
7. illumination; person; church; ministry; Holy Spirit; caught; trespass; spiritual; restore; gentleness; yourself; tempted
8. separate; believers; fellowship; problems; indication; problem ourselves
9. the Helper; nature; following; helping; problems; Love

Chapter Seventeen: Ten Things We Can Do to Get Free of the Religious Spirit

1. We could take the list and replace true intimacy with the Lord with more religious activity.
2. We need humility and God's grace to draw closer to Him rather than to create activity that pulls us away.
3. Personal notes in the chart below will reflect the reader's interaction with the Holy Spirit but may contain some of the following:

Guideline to draw close to God	Scripture (from the text OR ones that come to mind)	Personal notes
1. Develop a secret relationship with the Lord	John 5:44	Where do I want others to notice my spiritual disciplines or religious activity? Where do I seek glory from people rather than the glory of my God?
2. Pray that the same love with which the Father loved the Son would be in you	John 17:26	Have I prayed for the same love with which the Father loved Jesus to be in me? Have I asked Him to replace religious duty with love? Are my good works rooted in duty and not love?
3. Study to show thyself approved unto God and not people	2 Tim. 2:15; Luke 16:15	Do I study the Word so that others may see my knowledge or acknowledge my position? Have I departed in any way from the Spirit of Truth that leads to the truth of Jesus and not myself? Do I try to justify myself to others? Am I esteemed or detested in the sight of God?

4.	Spend quality time alone with the Lord each day	Possible answer: Matt. 6:6	How much time do I spend with God vs. any other individual? Am I motivated by guilt to spend more time with Him, or am I driven by my desire to spend time with Him continually?
5.	Seek to hear the voice of the Lord every day	John 10:27	How easy is it for me to hear the Lord's voice? Is my time with the Lord "quality time"? How would I measure the quality of the communication the Lord and I have each day? Do I seek Him in a meaningful way? Do I seek Him even above His words?
6.	Ask the Lord to give you the love for your neighbors that He has for them	Possible answer: Luke 10:27	How pure is my witness and ministry in terms of a motivation of love for others? Does my love for the Lord, first and foremost, come through my testimony and interaction? Do I love God more than those closest to me?
7.	Seek to turn your criticisms into intercession	Matt. 6:21	Is prayer my first response when I see something wrong? Do I pray for grace for others, especially for those who irritate me? Do I invest in prayer for others? Do I truly love them? Has God trusted me with the ministry of truth and the authority to witness? Have I been successful in turning former enemies into friends?
8.	Continually ask the Lord to see His glory	2 Cor. 3:18	How easy is it for me to see God's glory? Am I being changed into His image? Is doctrine something I follow or has it become my nature? Do I believe just in my mind, or do I believe in my heart?
9.	Keep as one of your highest goals to manifest the sweet aroma of the knowledge of God	Possible answer: 2 Cor. 2:14	Have I asked the Lord not to send me anywhere that His manifest presence is not going to be with me? Do I

	in every place		truly want to only be where God is? Is my behavior always befitting the presence of my King?
10.	When you have failed to do any of the things listed above properly, ask forgiveness	Phil. 3:13-14	Do I forget what I have done in the past by truly repenting? Do I turn from my sins and let the Lord's forgiveness cleanse me? Am I one that presses toward the mark of the high calling of God in Christ Jesus?

4. replace; source; spiritual life; true repentance; grace; performance; humility; pride
5. loving; loving; neighbors; discipline; obedience; love; need; desire; recognition; acceptance
6. manifestation; Tree; Knowledge; Good; Evil; looked; themselves; poison; deadly; deadly poison
7. Christ-centered; ourselves; performance
8. joining; work; cross; Christ; own; ourselves; crosses daily; glory; self-abasement; virtue; sacrifices; accomplished; He
9. false
10. false
11. true
12. false
13. false
14. true
15. true
16. true
17. true
18. false
19. true
20. false
21. To see Him, to abide in Him, and to reveal Him. When the Lamb enters the throne room, the elders cast their crowns at His feet.
22. Since the whole of creation was created through Him and for Him, we all have a Jesus-sized hole in our soul. Nothing will ever satisfy the longing of the human heart or bring peace except a genuine relationship with Christ Jesus. Therefore, religious activity will not fill that hole. It will actually repulse people. When Jesus is lifted up, however, people will find what they have been longing for and will be drawn to Him.
23. Unstoppable living waters begin to flow out of our innermost beings. When we join our water with the waters of others, it will become a great river of life in the earth. Those who drink from it will never be thirsty again. The more we get free of the religious spirit, the purer and cleaner these waters will be.